S. HRG. 113–156

POLITICAL, ECONOMIC, AND SECURITY SITUATION IN NORTH AFRICA

HEARING

BEFORE THE

SUBCOMMITTEE ON NEAR EASTERN AND SOUTH AND CENTRAL ASIAN AFFAIRS

OF THE

COMMITTEE ON FOREIGN RELATIONS UNITED STATES SENATE

ONE HUNDRED THIRTEENTH CONGRESS

FIRST SESSION

NOVEMBER 21, 2013

Printed for the use of the Committee on Foreign Relations

Available via the World Wide Web: http://www.gpo.gov/fdsys/

U.S. GOVERNMENT PRINTING OFFICE

86–355 PDF   WASHINGTON : 2014

For sale by the Superintendent of Documents, U.S. Government Printing Office
Internet: bookstore.gpo.gov   Phone: toll free (866) 512–1800; DC area (202) 512–1800
Fax: (202) 512–2104   Mail: Stop IDCC, Washington, DC 20402–0001

CONTENTS

POLITICAL, ECONOMIC, AND SECURITY SITUATION IN NORTH AFRICA

THURSDAY, NOVEMBER 21, 2013

U.S. SENATE,
SUBCOMMITTEE ON NEAR EASTERN AND
SOUTH AND CENTRAL ASIAN AFFAIRS,
COMMITTEE ON FOREIGN RELATIONS,
Washington, DC.

The subcommittee met, pursuant to notice, at 2:16 p.m., in room SD–419, Dirksen Senate Office Building, Hon. Tim Kaine (chairman of the subcommittee) presiding.

Present: Senators Kaine and Risch.

OPENING STATEMENT OF HON. TIM KAINE, U.S. SENATOR FROM VIRGINIA

Senator KAINE. Let me call this hearing to order. This is the Subcommittee on Near Eastern, South and Central Asian Affairs of the Senate Foreign Relations Committee.

I want to welcome two panels of excellent witnesses before us today to address political, economic, and security situation and developments in North Africa. We have two wonderful panels. I indicated to our first panel for a few seconds that we have had an interesting day on the floor, and there will be some more votes later today.

The ranking member, Senator Risch, has invited witnesses to participate as well, and we will likely be in and out during the hearing, but I think it is a good idea to go ahead and get started.

What I will do is give some opening comments, and then I will turn it to the witnesses and ask them to comment for about 5 minutes each, and then we will get into some Q&A, and then we will repeat with the second panel the same basic format, allowing other Senators who are here to ask questions as well.

This is my first hearing as chair of this subcommittee. I was the chairman of the International Development Subcommittee until late July, and then with the change in the membership of the FRC occasioned by the election of Senator Ed Markey, there was a switching in the committee chairs, and I am very excited to tackle this important region as is described here in this building from Marrakesh to Bangladesh.

I am excited to begin my chairmanship with a hearing on North Africa within that very broad and probably unmanageably broad scope of real estate in North Africa. We sometimes pay a little less attention to it than I think we should, and I wanted to begin here, and especially in a propitious way since King Mohammed VI of

Morocco is visiting the White House this week, I thought it was a good thing to do and coincident with his visit.

Three years ago, a young Tunisian unleashed a wave of mass political protest and change across North Africa and the broader Middle East, and also across the world. The Arab Spring has affected each of the countries of North Africa that we will discuss today. Morocco and Algeria have maintained basic political continuity during the Arab Spring. We will likely hear about some significant security status and political reform status about each of those countries today.

Tunisia and Libya have undergone fundamental and at times violent political change. Tunisia is participating in a national dialogue, and Tunisians seem generally committed to a democratic process, but in each of these countries there is significant work to do.

There are regional debates among these four countries about governance, accountability, the transparency of reforms, the effectiveness of governmental programs, economic liberalization and the role of religion and military in public life.

While the political and societal debates will go on for a long time, as they do here, the deterioration of security conditions recently has raised important questions and has raised the stakes certainly for local citizens and communities, and also for the United States and our interests. Violent extremist groups appear to be exploiting porous borders in the region and the weaknesses of security forces across North Africa. Al Qaeda in the Islamic Maghreb, AQIM, its affiliates and breakaway factions, and movements referring to themselves as Ansar al-Sharia are also capitalizing on divisive and entity issues, as well as popular frustrations with the slow pace of reforms in these transitional states.

AQIM at this point—we will have testimony about this—does not appear to pose an imminent threat to the United States outside of North and West Africa, but we are all concerned about its capacity to strike at civilian populations, at allied nations, and at United States and other Western interests, and also the role of these groups in regional arms trafficking and ties to other extremist organizations. I know we have witnesses who are very well prepared to talk about this today.

Since late 2010, U.S. policy has sought to encourage greater political openness and participation in North Africa while not undermining other foreign policy priorities, especially the efforts to combat terrorism. I want to hear about that balance.

In the budget environment, which is very challenging—I am on the budget committee as well—we are engaged in a budget conference which, if it works, would be the first example of a successful budget conference in a divided Congress since 1986. But one of the realities about the budget conference that we all grapple with is resource limitations. So large increases in U.S. assistance packages are not realistic at the current time.

I want to hear about programs, especially from the USAID perspective, policies and tools to address challenges in North Africa that do not come with high dollar figures but rely on innovation and smart investments, and how we are coordinating and leveraging those investments together with our international partners.

A few words about each of the countries in the region.

Morocco remains a staunch counterterrorism and security partner. We have a free trade agreement with Morocco, and Virginia ports, just to use my own State as an example, have strong business partnerships in Morocco. King Mohammad VI's visit with the President tomorrow is an important one to ratify and continue to express appreciation for a long-standing alliance that goes back into the 1770s. Senator Menendez and I sent a letter to the President this week encouraging the President to continue to build upon this relationship. I see opportunities with Morocco potentially as a positive example for the way the United States engages the rest of the region.

The United States has a strong dialogue with Algeria. We want to hear about the Algerian agenda. I know our relationship with Algeria is improving, especially as we face the common challenges and enemy of the AQIM. I would love to hear about ways from these witnesses' perspectives about how the Moroccan-Algerian relationship could be improved. There are economic opportunities being lost every day as a result of that tension, and that would, of course, mean addressing the long-disputed territories in the western Sahara.

Tunisia sought, sadly, to high-profile political assassinations in 2013, but the citizens still have high hopes for successful democratic transition. The Islamist Party, Al Nehadi, is engaging in what appears to be real political and democratic dialogue, the National Dialogue. We will hear about that. Secular and Islamist tensions persist, and powerful trade unions remain an effective regulator of the political process. I am anxious to hear about the prospects of the success of that dialogue, and United States programs to foster Tunisia's democratic process.

Libya is, obviously, a very, very vexing challenge, as this Nation knows so very well. The lack of security is threatening prospects for any real political process. We will hear, in our second panel, from a witness who is an expert on Libya—who is actually just back from Libya—Fred Wehrey from the Carnegie Institute, landed just yesterday, where he has been studying the militias, and we are looking forward to hearing that testimony.

Libya is different in that it does not need a lot of financial assistance. It has ample natural resources. But Libya needs capacity-building and training. Militias need to be disarmed, which is a huge task, and we are worried about porous borders and weapons proliferation, arms finding their way to Egypt, Gaza, and Syria.

I know the United States, along with international partners, is working on a comprehensive security assistance program, and we will hear about that.

Of course, we cannot talk about Libya without mentioning the tragedy at Benghazi on September 11, 2012. Four brave American public servants were killed. There has been a lot of attention on that. There has been a lot of effort to affix blame and also, and more importantly, an effort to learn what went wrong and what we can do to improve the safety of our Embassy and security personnel not only in North Africa but around the world.

I have been happy as a member of the Foreign Relations Committee to work on efforts with the Department of State to implement some of the recommendations of the Accountability Review Board to make sure that we can continue to carry out vigorous and aggressive diplomacy, but also to take the steps that we need to keep our embassy personnel safe.

We need to reward those and protect those and support those who do what Ambassador Chris Stevens and his colleagues were doing there. They believed in improving the livelihood of Libyans and promoting U.S. interests, and they felt that those were consistent, not inconsistent. Ambassador Stevens had so many close friends in the State Department and in Virginia. Dr. William Lawrence, who is on our second panel, was a close friend, and we look forward to hearing from him.

So, this is about our current status in North Africa and what our policies and orientation should be going forward. We want to break down barriers in the region. We want to hear about economic opportunities and the potential for economic integration, and we also want to talk about other initiatives such as the Trans-Sahara Counterterrorism Partnership which works with 10 countries in west North Africa, including Tunisia, Morocco, and Algeria.

I will reserve opening statements for Senator Risch for when he arrives and move right to the panel. Let me now introduce the first panel to you.

Ambassador Richard Schmierer is the Acting Principal Deputy Assistant Secretary of State in the Bureau of Near Eastern Affairs. He served as Ambassador to Oman and is the Deputy Assistant Secretary of State for Iraq. He began his diplomatic career in 1980 and has served all over Europe and the Middle East.

Ms. Amanda Dory currently serves as the Deputy Assistant Secretary of Defense for African Affairs in the Office of the Secretary of Defense. Prior to this, she served as the Deputy Assistant Secretary of Defense for Strategy and received a Presidential Rank Award for her work on the 2010 Quadrennial Defense Review. Her nongovernmental experience includes positions with the Carnegie Endowment for International Peace, Foreign Policy Magazine, and the Nuclear Non-Proliferation Project.

And finally on the first panel, Ms. Alina Romanowski currently serves as the Deputy Assistant Administrator for the Middle East Bureau of USAID. Since March 2013, she has fulfilled the duties of Assistant Administrator. She oversees a large and varied portfolio that provides about $1.5 billion annually in assistance across the Middle East region. Ms. Romanowski also served for 14 years at the Defense Department in senior positions involving the Near East and South Asia.

I would like to ask the witnesses to deliver opening statements in the order in which I introduced you, and following that we will begin questions and answers.

So, Mr. Schmierer, to you first.

STATEMENT OF RICHARD SCHMIERER, PRINCIPAL DEPUTY ASSISTANT SECRETARY OF STATE, NEAR EASTERN AFFAIRS, U.S. DEPARTMENT OF STATE, WASHINGTON, DC

Mr. SCHMIERER. Well, Chairman Kaine, thank you very much for the invitation to be here today, and it is a particular honor to appear here with my colleagues, Deputy Assistant Secretary for Defense Amanda Dory, and Deputy Assistant Administrator Alina Romanowski, with whom I enjoy working on a regular basis.

We welcome the opportunity to speak to you on the issues you have just outlined and certainly look forward to answering any questions that you or your colleagues may have.

I have a fuller statement which I asked to be submitted for the record.

Senator KAINE. Without objection.

Mr. SCHMIERER. And with your permission, I would like to just simply summarize my remarks.

As you have just indicated, North Africa, which is known in Arabic as the Maghreb, is a region of tremendous potential. It is the birthplace of the Arab Awakening, and it is currently undergoing a difficult but critical transformation. Tunisia pursues efforts to achieve the democratic promise of its 2011 revolution, as Libya continues to undertake its democratic transition while confronting numerous challenges on the political, security, and economic fronts. Morocco and Algeria have undertaken a more gradual reform process. They remain key regional sources of stability and have assumed increasingly important roles in our global effort to combat terrorism and extremism.

We continue to enjoy a very strong bilateral partnership with Morocco, a relationship that we look forward to strengthening during the visit of King Mohammed VI this week to Washington. This is an opportunity to discuss the best means of promoting security and prosperity in the region.

Under King Mohammed VI, the political system has gradually liberalized. A new constitution was adopted in 2011, and Morocco's first Islamist-led government won nationwide democratic elections. We will continue to support Morocco as it undertakes these important reforms.

In Algeria, Mr. Chairman, we have also built a strong relationship characterized by our shared interests to combat terrorism and facilitate greater regional stability. In addition, we are focused on developing a more robust economic partnership and supporting civil society development. We have encouraged Algeria to continue to expand its regional leadership role to stabilize neighboring states, which struggle to address terrorist threats, loose weapons, and porous borders.

Our continued engagement in Libya is absolutely essential, Mr. Chairman. It is in our national security interest to ensure that Libya becomes a stable and democratic partner. Faced with daily violence, the Libyan Government has been unable to address the country's overlapping challenges. We stand ready to support future elections in Libya, as well as constitutional drafting and national dialogue efforts necessary for security and governance to take root.

As a part of this effort, we have agreed to train 5,000 to 8,000 members of a general purpose force with Italy and the United

Kingdom to be the core of a new Libyan Army. We are also in the process of beginning to implement a global security contingency fund border security program to provide technical expertise, training and equipment to build Libya's border security capacity.

Yet, security is only part of the solution. We also welcome the opportunity with our partners to help the Libyan Government build its governance capacity.

And finally, Mr. Chairman, we continue to view Tunisia as one of the region's best hopes for a successful transition to democracy. The assassination of an opposition politician in July led to calls for the dissolution of the government. Civil society mediators have been facilitating negotiations between the government and the opposition. We are encouraging Tunisian leaders across the political spectrum to continue efforts to finalize a constitution that respects the universal rights of all Tunisians and to set an election date. It also remains a top priority to help bolster Tunisian security capacity.

This region remains vital to protecting our national interests as we look to maintain relationships with key allies and to nudge nascent democracies through difficult transitions, with the aim of promoting stability and countering extremist threats.

Chairman Kaine, thank you for the opportunity to testify before you today. I look forward to answering your questions.

[The prepared statement of Mr. Schmierer follows:]

PREPARED STATEMENT OF RICHARD SCHMIERER

Chairman Kaine, Ranking Member Risch, members of the subcommittee, it is an honor to appear before you to provide background on U.S. engagement and policy in North Africa. As you know, this is an area of strategic importance to the Obama administration.

I am also pleased to appear before you today with USAID Deputy Assistant Administrator Alina Romanowski and Deputy Assistant Secretary for Defense Amanda Dory. I have had the pleasure of working closely with both Ms. Romanowski and Ms. Dory for some time to further our foreign policy objectives in the region and to protect our national security interests. We welcome the opportunity to speak to you today and look forward to answering any questions you may have regarding North Africa and our policy.

Mr. Chairman, as you know, North Africa—known in Arabic as the Maghreb—is a region of tremendous potential. The birthplace of the Arab Awakening, it is currently undergoing a difficult but critical transformation. Tunisia continues efforts to achieve the democratic promise of its 2011 revolution, even as it faces significant security and economic challenges. Libya continues to undertake a democratic transition following a successful revolution, yet confronts numerous challenges on the political, security, and economic fronts. Libya struggles with the daily threat of violence posed by a lack of security and political consensus, yet our continued engagement there is absolutely essential. Morocco and Algeria have undertaken more gradual reform processes. They remain key regional sources of stability and have assumed increasingly important roles in our global effort to combat terrorism and extremism. At the same time, the strained relationship between Algeria and Morocco also limits regional cooperation and development, which is essential if any regional bodies are to evolve into credible forces for regional stability—in the Maghreb and the Sahel.

MOROCCO

We continue to enjoy a very strong bilateral relationship with Morocco, focused on promoting regional stability, supporting democratic reform efforts, countering violent extremism, and strengthening trade and cultural ties. Morocco—a major non-NATO ally since 2004—is one of our closest counterterrorism partners in the region, and an active member of the Global Counterterrorism Forum. During its current term on the U.N. Security Council, Morocco is playing an important role in international efforts to end the Syrian civil war. We also enjoy a strong economic relationship; a bilateral free trade agreement that entered into force in 2006 has increased bilateral trade by 244 percent.

We look forward to strengthening this bilateral relationship during this week's visit of King Mohammed VI to Washington. This is an opportunity for the United States to reaffirm our close strategic partnership with Morocco and to discuss the best means of promoting security and prosperity in the region. In particular, we look forward to deepening our consultations on regional issues, and will stress our shared priorities in Mali, Syria, the Maghreb, and the Sahel. We look forward to continuing our conversations at the next session of the U.S.-Morocco Strategic Dialogue. Unfortunately, Secretary Kerry had to postpone the Dialogue in order to attend urgent negotiations in Geneva in mid-November, but we look forward to rescheduling the Strategic Dialogue soon.

Under King Mohammed VI, the Moroccan political system has gradually liberalized; the King founded the Arab world's first truth and reconciliation commission— to investigate abuses that occurred during his father's reign—and expanded women's rights. A new constitution was adopted in 2011, and Morocco's first Islamistled government won nationwide democratic elections, but much progress remains to be made on implementing the guarantees and institutions including increasing engagement of its citizens, under the new constitution. We have a robust dialogue with the Moroccan Government on human rights and ways in which we can support the ongoing process of political reform.

We will continue to support Morocco as it undertakes these important reform efforts. Our bilateral assistance—roughly $31 million in FY 2013—focuses on promoting economic, political, and social reforms; deepening our security partnership by supporting modern military and law enforcement agencies; promoting export control and antiterrorism as well as countering violent extremism efforts; developing a professional criminal justice system; and encouraging broad-based economic growth that provides expanded opportunities for women and youth. Our flagship assistance program has been Morocco's $698 million Millennium Challenge Corporation (MCC) compact, which closed in September and focused on agriculture, fisheries, and artisans.

With regards to the Western Sahara, we support the United Nations-led process designed to bring about a peaceful, sustainable, and mutually acceptable solution to the Western Sahara question. We also support the work of the U.N. Secretary General's Personal Envoy for the Western Sahara and urge the parties to work toward a resolution.

ALGERIA

Algeria and the United States have built a strong bilateral relationship, characterized by our shared interests to combat terrorism and facilitate greater stability in the region. We are also focused on developing a more robust trade and economic partnership and supporting the development of civil society groups. Unfortunately, Secretary Kerry had to postpone the U.S.-Algeria Strategic Dialogue in order to attend urgent negotiations in Geneva earlier this month, and we look forward to rescheduling it soon.

Algeria has made steady and consistent progress on human rights and political transparency over the past 20 years. We are encouraging the government to create space for a more vibrant civil society and inclusive democratic process through supporting small civil society initiatives, such as funding training for local election monitors. We also aim to increase educational exchanges with young Algerians, including promoting English language learning.

The wealth from Algeria's significant hydrocarbon reserves has empowered the state at the expense of overall economic development, dampening employment, and the development of human capital. We continue to encourage Algeria to make market-oriented changes that expand job opportunities and increase its attractiveness to foreign direct investment. With that in mind, we are working to strengthen our trade relationship with Algeria, and are seeking to reactivate the 2001 Trade and Investment Framework Agreement. General Electric recently signed a $2.7 billion deal to provide gas turbines to Algeria, an example of the benefits of our efforts to promote U.S. business in Algeria. This deal alone will help create 4,000 American jobs.

We have encouraged Algeria to continue to expand its regional leadership role to help stabilize neighboring states, which struggle to address terrorist threats, loose weapons, and porous borders. Algeria's experience fighting an Islamist insurgency during the 1990s resulted in a well-equipped and battle-hardened military that constitutes the strongest counterterrorism force in the region. We will continue to encourage Algeria to use this expertise to train and partner with less experienced militaries and law enforcement units in the region to help ensure greater stability in the Sahel and Maghreb. Algeria has purchased U.S. equipment via Direct Commercial Sales, but has not overcome its significant reservations about the Foreign Military Sales program. We also support countering violent extremist efforts seeking to provide positive alternatives for at risk youth.

LIBYA

Since the 2011 revolution, Libya has faced significant political and security challenges. Yet our continued engagement there is absolutely essential. It is in our national security interest to ensure Libya becomes a stable and democratic partner capable of addressing regional security challenges and advancing our shared interests. A successful democratic transition will result in a strategic partner with significant energy reserves and the ability to exert a positive and stabilizing influence in a critical region.

Mr. Chairman, let me assure you that, despite its challenges, Libya is making progress. In the first credible, transparent, and largely peaceful elections in a generation, Libyans elected a General National Congress (GNC) in July 2012, and the government continues to take steps toward establishing a constitution. More recently, the Prime Minister's staff, and the United Nations Support Mission in Libya (UNSMIL) have taken steps to move a national dialogue process forward to help resolve political differences. The Libyan Government and GNC have taken steps to pass a transitional justice law, which will help guide national justice and reconciliation efforts. The Justice Minister has also taken to heart recommendations for prison reform. The United States has signed memoranda of understanding with the Libyan Government to increase cooperation on education reform, cultural preservation, and chemical weapons destruction. In addition, 681 candidates for the constitutional drafting committee registered in October and November 2013. NATO recently agreed to respond positively to Prime Minister Zeidan's request for support in security sector capacity building.

Yet while the government enjoys democratic legitimacy, it lacks the ability to project its authority across the country or fulfill many core government functions. Faced with competing factions and the daily threat of violence, the Libyan Government and political actors have been unable to address the country's overlapping challenges. A political agreement is necessary to advance the National Dialogue and enable the constitution-drafting process to unfold, empowering the government to improve governance and establish security in the interim. The government must also work to demonstrate that Libya's vast natural resources will be used to benefit the entire Libyan population, and use those resources to promote economic growth. We stand ready to support future elections in Libya, as well as constitutional drafting and national dialogue efforts necessary for security and governance to take root.

After 42 years of dictatorship, Libya suffers from instability and poor governance due to weak institutions, wide, porous borders, huge stockpiles of loose conventional weapons, and the presence of militias, some of whom have extremist ties. Without capable police and national security forces that work with communities, security, and justice sector institutions struggle to fulfill their mandate, and rule of law is undermined, enabling criminality, illicit trade, and frustration to grow. The government has struggled to wrest power and influence from militias, which continue to wield local and regional power; the absence of political consensus on the way forward hampers these efforts. In a direct challenge to the weak central government, various actors—including federalist, militia, and ethnic groups—have blocked production and exports at many of Libya's onshore facilities.

Our assistance efforts are focused on providing support in order to build the capacity of Libyan institutions to face these challenges and to ensure a peaceful transition to democracy. Since Libya is a wealthy nation, we view our assistance in these areas as seed money intended to jump-start and unlock Libyan investment in programs that ultimately the government must own. To improve the government's ability to establish stability throughout the country, we responded positively to a request this spring from Prime Minister Zeidan that we help to train a General Purpose Force (GPF) to be the core of a new Libyan Army. At the U.K.-hosted G8 summit in June, we pledged to train a 5,000–8,000 member GPF, prompting the U.K. and Italy to pledge to train 2,000 members each. The GPF assistance will be paid for by the Libyan Government through a Foreign Military Sales case which will need to be congressionally notified.

Border security is also a critical U.S. and international concern in Libya. Libya's uncontrolled borders permit the flow not only of destabilizing Qadhafi-era conventional weapons, but also violent extremists throughout North Africa, the Middle East, and the Sahel. The flow of these foreign fighters has increased since the fall of Qadhafi and was highlighted by the January 2013 attack in Amenas, Algeria. We are in the process of beginning to implement a Global Security Contingency Fund (GSCF) border security program to provide technical expertise, training, and limited equipment to build Libya's interministerial border security capacity to address security along its southern land border. This program includes training and equipment programming for Libya's neighbors—Chad, Niger, and Algeria—to improve border security cooperation with Libya. In addition, we have a GSCF training and equipment program to build special operations forces capacity.

Libya's European partners also provide significant amounts of security and justice sector assistance to Libya. We ensure that our assistance complements their efforts and responds to the security needs identified by the Libyan Government. Given constraints on Libyan capacity to accept international assistance, a difficult security environment, and persistent instability, implementing pledged assistance is challenging, and often takes more time than expected. If we continue to help Libya build its capacity, however, these challenges can lessen.

We have made commitments to support Libya's security sector with the knowledge that enhanced security is only part of the solution. We also welcome the opportunity, with our international partners, to help the Libyan Government build its governance capacity. We support the Libyan Government and civil society groups in their work to construct the foundations of a new democratic society in Libya through capacity-building programs for nascent civil society organizations, political parties, the GNC, selected local councils, and media institutions, and work with partners to engage women and youth as active participants in the democratic transition.

TUNISIA

Tunisia remains one of the Middle East and North Africa's best hopes for a successful transition to democracy. Efforts continue to finalize a new constitution and set a date for democratic elections for President and Parliament. Tunisia's constituent assembly—tasked with drafting the constitution—completed a fourth draft in June. This draft incorporates human rights norms, including equality between women and men, and respect for rule of law.

As with all transitions, of course, there are also challenges. This year, there have been two assassinations of opposition politicians: one in February and one in July.

Following the July assassination, there were widespread, peaceful demonstrations calling for the dissolution of the government. Civil society mediators have since been facilitating negotiations between the government and the opposition, with the goal of implementing a political transition roadmap. We are encouraging Tunisian leaders across the political spectrum to continue their efforts to finalize a constitution that respects the human rights of all Tunisians and to set a date for credible and transparent elections so the Tunisian people can determine their country's future.

As we saw with the unfortunate killings of politicians and most recently the attempted suicide attacks in tourist areas, violent extremists continue to seek to derail the country's efforts to transition to democracy peacefully and successfully. Over the past year, the Tunisian Government has taken a more aggressive stance against extremism, by raiding weapons caches and undertaking an operation to root out terrorists in the country's western region. In late August, the Government of Tunisia designated Ansar al Sharia—Tunisia (AAS–T) a terrorist organization, and the security forces have since banned the group's activities and made several high level arrests.

This approach is not without its challenges. The Tunisian military and security forces require additional training and equipment to counter the newly evolving terrorist threat. Improving and deepening our security cooperation is of top importance in our bilateral relationship. We have bolstered our assistance to help Tunisia reform its criminal justice sector to improve its ability to protect Tunisians and foreigners alike, as well as confront domestic and regional security challenges. For example, in September 2013, our two countries signed a letter of agreement to expand programming to reform and improve the capacity of the police and corrections officials. The other challenge is ensure that this aggressive, security based approach is balanced with proven methods to prevent recruitment into violent extremist organizations. We are working with Tunisia to explore ways to provide at-risk groups with alternatives and preventing further marginalization or disconnection of these groups.

We also continue to provide foreign assistance via a number of mechanisms to support Tunisia's transition from dictatorship to a prosperous democratic country. On the economic front, we are helping Tunisia expand economic growth and opportunity to all citizens, and encouraging it to undertake market-oriented and institutional reforms. Our focus with existing programs has been to spur job creation and provide entrepreneurship training as well as to enhance access to finance for small and medium enterprises. At the same time, we continue to fund programs that support Tunisia's democratic political processes and plan to support international and domestic elections observation missions.

PROTECTING OUR INTERESTS

Chairman Kaine, Ranking Member Risch, and members of the subcommittee, I want to thank you for the opportunity to testify before you today. Certainly, we are aware that our budgets are facing increasing pressure, but this region remains vital to protecting our national interests, as we look to maintain relationships with key allies and to nudge nascent democracies through difficult transitions, with the hope of promoting stability and countering extremist threats in the Middle East and Africa. With careful, targeted assistance, and smart diplomatic engagement, we are successfully advancing our key strategic interests.

Thank you again for your time and attention. I look forward to answering your questions.

Senator KAINE. Thank you very much.
Ms. Dory.

STATEMENT OF AMANDA DORY, DEPUTY ASSISTANT SECRETARY OF DEFENSE, AFRICAN AFFAIRS, U.S. DEPARTMENT OF DEFENSE, WASHINGTON, DC

Ms. DORY. Chairman Kaine, I am pleased to appear before this subcommittee for the first time to provide an update on the security situation in North Africa and the Department of Defense's engagement strategy in the region. DOD is committed to working closely with the State Department to enhance U.S. Government security assistance to build the capacity of North African security forces. Our strategic approach recognizes that developing strong and responsive defense institutions can support regional stability, allowing partner militaries to operate under civilian authority while respecting the rule of law and international human rights.

Each of the four countries under discussion today faces a differing array of political, economic, and governance challenges as a result of the political upheavals that you have already cited. North African countries will continue to face security challenges, and addressing those challenges will take time, particularly in the case of Libya.

Our goals are to focus on long-term institution-building and regional cooperation in coordination with other countries, to be supportive of host nation requests, and to maintain a limited and effective U.S. military footprint in the region.

In Morocco, Algeria, and Tunisia, DOD maintains close military-to-military ties with our respective senior military and civilian counterparts. Our shared security goals include countering terrorism and enhancing cross-border security. We regularly engage with counterpart defense institutions in each of the three governments on a bilateral basis to ensure alignment of goals and prioritization of security cooperation activities.

In addition to bilateral engagements, the Trans-Sahara Counterterrorism Partnership, TSCTP, is a multiyear regional program that brings State Department, Department of Defense, and USAID together to build the capacity and resilience of the governments and communities in the Sahel and Maghreb to address the threat of violent extremist organizations.

A few quick remarks on each of the countries.

With Libya, Libya remains a country with a very difficult democratic transition. Militia violence and consequent retributive attacks continue within the country. The Libyan Government is unable to control its borders, contributing to instability from Mali westward within the Sahel. The Department of Defense is prioritizing assistance to focus on building Libyan security institutional capacity and on improving the government's ability to counter terrorism, and to secure and destroy its chemical weapons stockpiles.

On the latter point, our chemical weapons abatement program with Libya is on schedule to eliminate remaining Libyan chemical weapons by the end of 2013 in accordance with Libya's international commitments.

And thanks to congressional support, this fiscal year the United States will work with Libya to develop their capacity to conduct counterterrorism operations and border security, particularly along the southern land border.

Additionally, in response to requests from the Prime Minister, we have offered to provide General Purpose Force military training, as already mentioned. The training is intended to help the government build the military it requires to protect government institutions and maintain order. This effort builds on the G8 summit announcement that focused on the expansion of support for Libya's security sector.

In Tunisia, Tunisia's military deserves tremendous credit for supporting and protecting the population during Tunisia's democratic transition. The government continues to grapple with the threat of violent extremism. Our assistance to the security sector focuses on counterterrorism support, border security training, and a continuation of long-standing programs such as the International Military Education and Training Program and Foreign Military Financing.

Algeria has been a critical security partner in countering regional violent extremist organizations. In particular, it is a linchpin in the struggle against Al Qaeda in the Islamic Maghreb, AQIM, and its affiliates. The January 2013 terrorist attack against the In Amenas oil facility highlighted the growing transnational threats in the region. The Algerian military continues to conduct successful interdiction operations on its southern border against AQIM and affiliates. Additionally, Algeria provides training and equipment assistance to its neighbors, contributing to broader regional efforts. DOD engages with Algeria across a range of activities, to include IMAT information-sharing and exercises.

With Morocco, the United States and the Kingdom of Morocco share a long history of bilateral relations. Morocco has been a strong partner in the struggle against terrorism. The visit of the King this week has already been referenced. The Secretary of Defense and Secretary of State had an excellent meeting with him yesterday to discuss shared concerns, and our long-standing security cooperation with the Moroccans continues.

In conclusion, thank you for the chance to discuss today U.S. military cooperation in the Maghreb as it supports broader U.S. foreign policy, and I look forward to your questions.

[The prepared statement of Ms. Dory follows:]

PREPARED STATEMENT OF AMANDA DORY

Chairman Kaine, Ranking Member Risch, and distinguished members of the subcommittee, I am pleased to appear before you to update you on the security situation in North Africa and the Department of Defense's engagement strategy in the region in coordination with other interagency partners.

INTRODUCTION

The Department of Defense is committed to working closely with the Department of State to enhance U.S. Government security assistance to build the capacity of North African security forces. Our strategic approach recognizes that developing strong and responsive defense institutions can support regional stability, allowing partner militaries to operate under civilian authority while respecting the rule of law and international human rights.

The effects of the Arab Awakening in North Africa continue to reverberate within the region and beyond its borders into the Sahelian states of sub-Saharan Africa. Libya remains a key source of instability in North Africa and the Sahel. Thus, the Department of Defense is working closely with its interagency colleagues and partner nations to assist the Libyan Government in training its security forces and strengthening Libyan Government institutions.

In Morocco, Algeria, and Tunisia, the Department of Defense maintains close military-to-military ties with respective senior military and civilian Ministry of Defense counterparts. All three countries are committed to a security dialogue and partnership with the United States, and they share our goals of countering terrorism and enhancing cross-border security. We engage with the three governments on a bilateral basis every 12–18 months to ensure our shared security goals are aligned and U.S. Government security assistance is prioritized accordingly.

The negative effects of terrorism and growing violent extremism have been experienced by all our partners in North Africa, and have underscored to them the gravity of the threat and the value of partnering with the United States and the international community to address shared security challenges, which extend beyond the Maghreb. For example, each country is cognizant that its nationals are traveling to Syria to support violent extremists fighting against the Syrian Government, and is aware of the danger to North African security if and when those fighters return.

To address regional instability in North Africa and the Sahel more broadly, the U.S. Government established, in 2005, the Trans-Sahara Counterterrorism Partnership (TSCTP). The TSCTP is a multiyear, regional program to build the capacity and resilience of the governments and communities in the Sahel and Maghreb to address the threat of violent extremist organizations. The TSCTP also provides a means to improve regional and international cooperation and information-sharing.

COUNTRY-BY-COUNTRY SECURITY ENVIRONMENT/DOD PROGRAMS

Libya

Libya remains a country in a difficult democratic transition, and the path to stability continues to be a challenging one for the weak government institutions in Tripoli. The recent kidnapping and release of Prime Minister Zeidan underscore the serious shortcomings in the Libyan security environment. Militia violence and consequent retributive attacks continue within the country. The Libyan Government is unable to control its borders, and weaponry smuggled from Libya is fueling instability from Mali westward within the Sahel. We and our Libyan partners are working on joint programs designed to address the needed skill sets of Libyan security forces to address these challenges adequately.

The Department of Defense is prioritizing its assistance to focus on building Libyan security institutional capacity and on improving the Libyan Government's ability to counter terrorism, counter weapons proliferation, and secure and destroy its chemical weapons stockpiles. Thanks to congressional support, the United States is working with Libya to develop their capacity to conduct counterterrorism operations via a $8.42M Section 1206 Special Operations Support company and medical training program; and a $7.75M Global Security Contingency Fund (GSCF) SOF company build program. DOD will also provide training for the larger interagency GSCF Under the joint State-DOD GSCF authority, we are also pursuing a $14.9M program to provide technical expertise, training, and limited equipment to build Libya's interministerial (i.e., MOD, MOI, and Customs) border security program ($14.9M) capacity to address security along its southern land border. This program includes training and equipping to build a border security company, and programming for Libya's neighbors—Chad, Niger, and Algeria—to improve border security cooperation with Libya. We remain hopeful that these projects will positively impact Libya's security situation.

An additional program that the United States is working with Libya is a $45 million chemical weapons abatement program at Waddan, Libya where we have installed a static detonation chamber, and a U.S. contractor is ramping up operations and is on schedule to eliminate remaining Libyan chemical weapons by the end of 2013 in accordance with Libya's international commitments.

In response to a request from Libyan Prime Minister Zeidan, the United States has offered to provide General Purpose Force military training for 5,000–8,000 personnel. This training effort is intended to help the government build the military it requires to protect government institutions and maintain order. It is one element of the targeted security programs the United States has provided to Libya since 2011, building on the February 2013 Paris Ministerial-level meeting on supporting Libya's security and justice sector needs and British Prime Minister Cameron's announcement at the G8 summit in June about expanding international support for Libya's security sector. The United Kingdom and Italy have also committed to train 2,000 Libyan General Purpose Forces personnel, each.

We expect the U.S.-led training to begin via FMS in the spring of 2014 at a U.S.-leased/run training facility in Bulgaria and to continue over a number of years based on cohort size and the pace of training. The Government of Libya has committed to fund this training program and provided initial financial deposits. The United States will work closely with Libya to ensure all candidates for training are properly vetted to ensure that they meet human rights standards in accordance with U.S. law.

All U.S. assistance will continue to be coordinated with the U.N. Support Mission in Libya (UNSMIL) and with European partners who have also offered substantial security sector assistance to the Government of Libya.

Tunisia

Tunisia's military deserves tremendous credit for supporting and protecting the population during Tunisia's democratic transition. More recently, following a series of terrorist attacks on the Tunisian military in the Chaambi Forest beginning in April 2013, as well as the assassination of two opposition political figures, the Tunisian Government continues to grapple with the threat of violent extremism. U.S. assistance to the security sector focuses on counterterrorism support, border security training, and a continuation of our longstanding Foreign Military Financing (FMF) and International Military Education and Training (IMET) programs.

The United States has provided technical assistance, equipment, and training to Tunisian Ministries and agencies to make them more effective in securing land border crossings, maritime borders, ports, and airport and seaport operations. U.S. assistance has also provided equipment and relevant training for inspection and/or detection equipment.

Maintenance and upgrade of existing equipment and the addition of critically needed procurements through FMF is a U.S. priority to help address the Ministry of Defense's (MOD's) broadened mission and to reinforce efforts to counter the growing threat of violent extremism. The United States is also assisting the Ministry with training through IMET funding, with an emphasis on enhancing strategic planning capabilities.

Algeria

Algeria has been a critical security partner in countering regional violent extremist organizations. Its strategic location in the Maghreb, and its long history combating domestic terrorism and violent extremism, make Algeria a linchpin in the struggle against Al Qaeda in the Islamic Maghreb (AQIM) and its affiliates and bringing stability to the region. The January 2013 terrorist attack against the In Amenas oil facility highlighted the growing transnational threats in the region. The Algerian military continues to conduct successful interdiction operations on its southern border against AQIM affiliates. Additionally, Algeria provides training and equipment assistance to its Sahel neighbors, contributing to broader regional efforts to curb violent extremist groups' transborder movement and activities.

As a result, the Department of Defense continues to expand engagement with Algeria in cooperation with other U.S. Government departments and agencies across a range of activities, to include information sharing and exercises. The Algerian Government is also interested in acquiring U.S. equipment for counterterrorism purposes. To address this interest, the Department of Defense is working to provide Algeria with equipment and training to enhance Government of Algeria defense capabilities. Algeria has acquired U.S. goods and services, equipment, and training via direct commercial sales since the 1980s, including a border security system from

Northrup Grumman and eight Lockheed C–130 transport aircraft. U.S. bilateral military engagement and sustained dialogue is also expanded through the IMET program, which is enhancing professionalization and modernization of Algeria's Armed Forces.

Morocco

From the beginning of his reign, King Mohammed VI has recognized that democratic political and economic reforms are needed. During the Arab Awakening, he continued to respond to popular demands for change from within Moroccan society. Nevertheless, the earlier terrorist bombing in Casablanca in 2003 was a strong signal that Morocco was not immune from violent extremism and the regional threats to stability in the Maghreb and Sahel. We anticipate that security cooperation will be one of many themes during the King's meeting at the White House tomorrow.

The United States and the Kingdom of Morocco share a long history of bilateral relations that is enduring and expansive. A major non-NATO ally, Morocco has been a strong partner in the struggle against terrorism, and our bilateral military and political cooperation is growing. Among the first Islamic countries to condemn publicly the attacks of September 11, 2001, Morocco provided forces in Desert Storm, Bosnia, and Kosovo. Additionally, Morocco is a strong contributor to global U.N. peacekeeping operations.

Our security cooperation programs with Morocco enhance Morocco's military professionalism through the International Military Education and Training program and help to increase Morocco's effectiveness and capabilities in the context of multilateral operations through provision of Foreign Military Financing and Excess Defense Articles. Additionally, U.S. Africa Command partners with Morocco to execute a robust program of Military-to-Military activities and joint military exercises, including AFRICAN LION—a significant joint and combined exercise on the continent. U.S. security support to Morocco has a cascade-like effect on the region as Morocco in turn provides assistance to more than 20 African countries through training and humanitarian assistance.

CONCLUSION

Each of the four countries under discussion today faces a differing array of political, economic, and governance challenges as a result of the political upheavals of the last several years in the region. North African countries will continue to face security challenges as a result, and addressing those challenges will take time, particularly in the case of Libya. Our goals are to focus on long-term institution building and regional cooperation in coordination with other countries, to be supportive of host government requests, and to maintain a small and effective U.S. military footprint in the region.

Thank you for your time and attention today. We appreciate your interest in, and support of, U.S. military cooperation in the Maghreb as it supports broader U.S. foreign policy and national security objectives in the region, and I will be pleased to answer any questions.

Senator KAINE. Thank you.
Ms. Romanowski.

STATEMENT OF ALINA ROMANOWSKI, DEPUTY ASSISTANT ADMINISTRATOR, MIDDLE EAST BUREAU, U.S. AGENCY FOR INTERNATIONAL DEVELOPMENT, WASHINGTON, DC

Ms. ROMANOWSKI. Chairman Kaine, thank you for the opportunity to appear before you today to discuss USAID's ongoing efforts to support U.S interests in North Africa.

As my colleagues have said, North Africa is a region of many possibilities and great importance, but also one that faces daunting challenges, especially in this transition period.

For the past 3 years, USAID has supported Morocco, Tunisia, and Libya as they write new constitutions, reform institutions, as they carry out credible and transparent elections, and as citizens advocate for increased political participation. Our programs target the development challenges that span North Africa, including high unemployment and the lack of economic growth, and work to address factors that push local populations toward violent extremism.

The Arab Awakening has been a regional phenomenon, but each country experiences it differently. So we have tailored our programs to each country's specific needs.

In Libya, USAID has supported the transition by developing governance institutions and building an emerging civil society. As Libyans begin to draft a new constitution, USAID is working to ensure that the Libyan people are engaged in that process.

We are also promoting women's empowerment by supporting programs that engage women in the political process, like a series of training programs where some women were provided internships with the High National Elections Commission, and these women were, in fact, permanently hired.

USAID is supporting women through economic growth programs that strengthen women entrepreneurs by providing business skills training and improving their access to finance through brokered relationships with financial institutions.

Tunisia remains one of the region's best hopes for a successful transition to democracy. USAID strongly supports the Tunisian people as they lay the foundation for economic prosperity that empowers a new generation, strengthens civil society, and solidifies the institutions of democracy.

To promote economic growth, we launched the Tunisian-American Enterprise Fund, a signature United States initiative that will invest in growing the Tunisian economy. Currently capitalized at $40 million, the Enterprise Fund is designed to develop the much-needed private sector in Tunisia, expand access to credit, and create opportunities for Tunisian small- and medium-sized businesses.

In 2012, USAID provided the provisional government a $100 million cash transfer that supported its short-term budget needs. USAID also subsidized the cost of a $485 million loan guarantee to help address Tunisia's longer term financing needs.

AID is encouraging job creation in high-impact, growing sectors of the economy like information communications technology. Our ICT program recently organized a job fair where 4,500 young Tunisians met with over 200 employers to discuss job opportunities. Additionally, our work in the ICT sector has generated over 2,400 new jobs for Tunisians.

USAID is also actively engaged in helping Tunisians build a peaceful and stable democratic political process. During Tunisia's historic October 2011 elections, USAID supported the only nationwide campaign targeting women voters, and also a get-out-the-vote campaign that focused on youth. For Tunisia's upcoming elections, USAID will support international and local monitoring activities.

For over 50 years, USAID and the Government of Morocco have had a strong bilateral relationship that continues today. This year, to support the ambitious political and economic reform goals of the Moroccan Government and respond to the needs of the Moroccan citizens, USAID has designed a new 5-year country development strategy. This is a focused plan to work side by side with the Government of Morocco, civil society, and the private sector to enhance the employability of Morocco's large youth demographic, improve the education system, strengthen the civil society organizations, and improve the credibility and transparency of political parties.

During this week's visit of Mohammed VI, we will launch this new strategy, reaffirming our long history of cooperation in promoting sustainable development in Morocco.

So in conclusion, during this time of transition, it is essential that AID continue its engagement with the region's people and their governments to build free, democratic, prosperous, and secure nations. This engagement is vital to countering extremist threats, maintaining relationships with key allies, and advancing key U.S. strategic interests.

Chairman Kaine, thank you very much, and I look forward to answering your questions today.

[The prepared statement of Ms. Romanowski follows:]

PREPARED STATEMENT OF ALINA L. ROMANOWSKI

Chairman Kaine, Ranking Member Risch, and members of the subcommittee, thank you for the opportunity to appear before you to discuss the political and economic situation in North Africa and USAID's ongoing efforts to support U.S interests in the region through our programs and assistance.

Over the last 30 years of my career, I have had the privilege to serve across four government agencies, focusing on the Middle East. I know firsthand that it is a region of many possibilities and great importance, but also one that faces daunting challenges, especially in this transition period. This is clearly illustrated in North Africa, where the Arab Awakening began. Tunisia—the country where in 2011 a single man's frustration and desperation with his economic situation touched off a chain of events that would topple governments around the region—continues to make progress along its path toward a successful transition to democracy. Similarly, in response to its citizens' calls for change, the Government of Morocco has laid out an important reform agenda of social and economic change and has taken steps toward a more inclusive government. In Libya, despite obvious setbacks and ongoing security challenges, Libyans have repeatedly expressed their deep desire to transform into a democracy, pushing forward with their constitutional drafting process and pushing back against unruly militias. As you can see, each of these countries' path to a more inclusive, responsive government, and ultimately to stability, varies.

Our continued and flexible engagement to support the efforts of the region's people and their governments to build free, democratic, prosperous, and secure nations is absolutely essential. For the past 3 years, USAID has supported these countries in transition as they write new constitutions and reform institutions, as they carry out credible and transparent elections, and as citizens advocate for increased political participation. Our programs also target the major development challenges that span North Africa, including the lack of economic growth, high unemployment and large youth demographics. A key component to the region's economic development and expansion is inclusive growth and opportunities for women and minorities. USAID programs focus on the engines of economic growth by supporting small- and medium-sized enterprises—especially those managed by women—through training, marketing assistance and building connections with financial institutions.

As these North African countries experience transition, USAID programs are on the forefront of undercutting structural factors that push and pull local populations toward violent extremism. We know that weak governments and chronic underdevelopment, coupled with marginalization of groups, create vulnerabilities to recruitment into violent extremist and terrorist groups. Connecting citizens with their government and providing economic opportunities is vital. Our governance programs highlight constituent outreach and civil society capacity-building to shape the foundations of democratic nations. USAID economic programs also work to provide educational and vocational opportunities for youth and other previously marginalized populations. Our work in Libya to bolster the General National Congress and connect marginalized communities in the south with Tripoli also helps reduce the risk of violent extremism. USAID also has programs specifically targeting those at risk for recruitment into violent extremist groups. For instance, in Morocco, we are working with at-risk youth to connect them with vocational education and their local government to better engage with their communities. Security and development, therefore, are interlinked—connecting citizens with their government, enabling government to respond to its citizens, and developing economic opportunities to help create secure environments.

The political transitions surging through North Africa and the Middle East have been a regional phenomenon. Yet the reality is that each country experiences it differently and continues to transition in its own way reflecting the distinct voices of its citizens. As USAID supports the efforts of people across North Africa to define their own futures, we have tailored our policies and programs to each country's specific needs and experiences.

LIBYA

Our assistance to Libya is an essential component of our continued engagement in the region. It is in our national security interest to see a successful democratic transition in Libya and ensure we have a partner that can address regional security challenges. As such, USAID assistance in Libya has focused on supporting democratic transition, developing governance institutions, an emerging civil society and an engaged citizenry, and promoting women's engagement in Libya's economic growth. Since June 2011, USAID's Office of Transition Initiatives (OTI) has been working with Libya's civil society and governing authorities to build an inclusive and accountable democratic government that reflects the will and needs of the Libyan people. USAID partners with civil society organizations, local media outlets, and interim governing authorities to support inclusive transitional political and justice processes, strengthen local initiatives to mitigate conflict that destabilizes the transition, and promote the development of effective, legitimate governance institutions. USAID continues to support fair and effective electoral, political and governing processes in Libya by providing technical assistance to the Libyan Government, including the High National Election Commission, the Judiciary, the General National Congress and elected local councils to help them fulfill their responsibilities and communicate more effectively with Libyan citizens.

USAID is also helping to strengthen the ability of civil society to engage fellow citizens and decisionmakers on key issues, such as transitional justice, reconciliation and working to promote the peaceful reintegration of former revolutionaries. As Libya moves toward the next milestone of drafting a new constitution, USAID is working with the government and civil society to ensure that the Libyan people are informed and engaged in the process. To support national reconciliation, USAID is bringing together local council, religious, tribal and other community leaders to discuss how they can help their communities resolve longstanding conflicts.

We are also working with local women's organizations to raise awareness about important issues to be addressed in the constitution, and to help Libyan women advocate for their rights during the constitution drafting process. This year, USAID supported a women's political leadership program to promote women's participation in the political process. After a series of training programs and workshops, the program participants were placed into internships with the High National Elections Commission (HNEC), the High Judicial Institute, General National Congress committees, and constituency offices. All those who interned at the HNEC were then hired as permanent staff.

Last year, USAID launched the War Wounded Project to strengthen the Government of Libya's ability to provide rehabilitative care to the tens of thousands of Libyans wounded and disabled in the effort to topple the Qadhafi regime. USAID provides training to staff in the Ministries of Health, Social Affairs and Wounded & Missing to build their leadership and management capacity. USAID's original investment of $1.5 million to the War Wounded Project has leveraged an additional $9 million contribution from the Government of Libya to establish Leadership Development Institutes that will provide ongoing technical, management, and leadership training to health sector staff. Additionally, USAID worked with the U.S.-Libya Business Association to encourage private sector contributions to support treatment of the war-wounded in Libya. For example, a combined contribution of $1.5 million from ConocoPhillips and General Electric continued a nursing support project initially funded by USAID.

To support inclusive economic growth in Libya, USAID's Women's Economic Empowerment Program is strengthening women entrepreneurs and women-owned small and medium enterprises by providing business skills training and networking opportunities, and by improving women's access to finance through brokered relationships with financial institutions. USAID is also providing U.S.-based diaspora entrepreneurs with seed capital and technical assistance through a business plan competition to help start or expand businesses in Libya.

TUNISIA

Tunisia remains one of the region's best hopes for a successful transition to democracy. USAID strongly supports the Tunisian people as they lay the foundation for a future of economic prosperity that empowers a new generation, strengthens civil society and solidifies the foundation of democracy.

The development and growth of a robust and inclusive private-sector-led economy in Tunisia is central to the success of Tunisia's long-term political and economic security as well as to U.S. interests in Tunisia and in the broader region. The Tunisian-American Enterprise Fund (TAEF), announced by President Obama in May 2011, is a signature U.S. initiative that will invest in the Tunisian economy to unlock the benefits of private-sector-led growth. Currently capitalized at $40 million, the TAEF will invest in small and medium enterprises to promote inclusive economic growth and employment. The TAEF will help address gaps in financing for entrepreneurs and small businesses that overwhelmingly drive Tunisia's private sector growth and encourage Tunisia to undertake market-oriented and institutional reforms.

In 2012, USAID provided a $100 million cash transfer that supported the short-term budget needs of the provisional government. Additionally, USAID subsidized the cost of a U.S. guarantee of a $485 million Tunisian sovereign bond to help address Tunisia's longer term external financing needs.

Encouraging job creation is another key element in USAID's support for Tunisia's economic growth. As such, USAID has developed programs that enhance and diversify the education and job skills necessary for a nation's economic growth. For example, in partnership with the University of Texas San Antonio, we are in the process of launching 24 university career centers at six college campuses across Tunisia to help college students and graduates not only look for work but develop their careers. These entrepreneurs, and the businesses they create, are the underpinning of a future vibrant economy in North Africa. Many of our programs encourage students to build skills specific to sectors of the economy that are growing, like information and communications technology (ICT).

USAID's programs are creating jobs in high-impact sectors. Specifically, our work with the ICT sector has generated over 2,400 jobs. In September, our ICT program organized a job fair in Tunis where 4,500 young Tunisians met with over 200 employers to discuss job opportunities and future careers. Additionally, USAID helped a Silicon Valley-trained native Tunisian open a small information technology business in the city of Sousee, then assisted in product marketing and business plan development and eventually helped him recruit over 75 young graduates to work at his company.

We are also helping Tunisians expand a more diverse and qualified workforce that is responsive to the country's needs. A USAID-funded partnership between the University of Colorado and the Advanced Institute of Technology Studies in Sidi Bouzid is preparing graduates to contribute to their communities through career training in water management, energy efficiency, and renewable energy technologies.

USAID is also actively engaged in helping Tunisians build a peaceful and stable democratic political process and institutions. Specific efforts by OTI have focused on encouraging broad participation in the political transition with a particular emphasis on youth and women's engagement and working with local organizations to identify and respond to community priorities. USAID-supported democracy and governance activities have included nationwide voter education campaigns aimed at getting youth to vote and the only nationwide campaign targeting women voters in the lead up to Tunisia's historic October 2011 elections. Our programs continue to help build the capacity of new democratic institutions and Tunisian civil society organizations. Moving forward, USAID will support monitoring activities, by both the international and local communities, of Tunisia's upcoming elections.

MOROCCO

For over 50 years, USAID and the Government of Morocco have had a strong bilateral relationship focused on promoting economic growth, improving educational opportunities and strengthening inclusive political participation and an active civil society. We also have worked together to make substantial improvements in the lives of Moroccan citizens, including significantly improving maternal and child health, constructing two major dams, transforming thousands of semiarid acres into productive use, and providing microfinance loans.

Despite impressive economic growth over the past few years, Morocco still faces many complex challenges, including few employment opportunities for youth and an overall literacy rate of only 55 percent. As recent political transition sweep the region, Morocco has experienced a quiet and gradual transformation. The Government of Morocco responded to the Arab Awakening by reforming the constitution and laying out an ambitious agenda of political, economic, and social reforms. Implementing this reform agenda, while maintaining stability and security throughout the country, is of utmost importance for Morocco's future development and prosperity.

To help the Government of Morocco achieve its stated reform goals and respond to the needs of Moroccan citizens, USAID has developed a new 5-year Country Development Cooperation Strategy (CDCS) for Morocco—a focused plan to work side by side with the Moroccan Government, civil society and the private sector to support progress toward key reforms. The new CDCS will focus on workforce development, increasing citizen participation in governance and improving primary educational achievement. During this week's visit of King Mohammed VI to Washington, DC, USAID and the Government of Morocco will celebrate the launch of USAID's CDCS, reaffirming our long history of cooperation and collaboration based on a common interest in promoting sustainable development in Morocco.

To enhance the employability of the country's large youth demographic, USAID will focus on improving the quality of and access to career services. We will facilitate partnerships between government ministries, Moroccan universities and technical institutes, as well as local NGOs and business associations to develop demand-driven workforce development services that reach a broad range of youth.

To increase citizen participation in governance, USAID will support the development of civil society organizations to develop their constituencies, form effective coalitions and develop policy recommendations. USAID will also continue to help political parties improve their credibility by increasing the transparency and accountability of their internal operations, developing platforms reflective of citizen needs and enhancing the involvement and leadership of youth and women in politics. Our efforts will provide long-term assistance targeting local branches of political parties to ensure citizen engagement at the grassroots level. By increasing the capacity of civil society to engage the government on behalf of citizens and facilitating the development of institutionalized mechanisms of civic participation in government decisionmaking, Morocco will be better situated to implement its reform agenda in a peaceful and sustainable fashion.

USAID's basic education program also plays a crucial role as Morocco strives to meet the needs of its growing youth population. In conjunction with Morocco's education reform effort, USAID will promote higher levels of educational attainment by targeting early grade reading. Poor reading skills increase children's chances that they will fall behind in school, setting the stage for future dropout. As such, these early grade reading programs are designed to improve early literacy and help curb primary grade dropout rates.

USAID also works to mitigate the drivers of violent extremism as part of supporting Morocco's peaceful reform agenda. Morocco has experienced several incidents of violent extremism over the past decade and, while low, risks of instability are heightened by societal factors that contribute to political and economic marginalization. In our countering violent extremism programming, we target areas of Morocco that suffer from high rates of illiteracy, school dropout, and unemployment, and are known breeding grounds for transnational terrorist networks. To reintegrate at-risk youth into mainstream society, we support nonformal education and vocational training, the provision of basic social services, career counseling, and job placement. Capacity-building for public and private social service providers targeting at-risk youth will increase sustainability and expand the reach of program activities.

Finally, I would like to conclude with Algeria, where USAID has a limited presence. While the United States is working to strengthen its bilateral relationship with Algeria, USAID currently has few programs there. Consistent with our regional efforts to combat terrorism and extremism, we are focusing on launching a program in Algeria that aims to reduce social and economic exclusion of at-risk Algerian youth.

CONCLUSION

USAID views our assistance programs in the North Africa region as an investment in protecting our national interests and in building long-term partnerships with the people and the governments of those countries. USAID programs will continue to provide the seeds for future innovation and technology, to advance economic prosperity and growth, and to strengthen regional stability and security. The countries and peoples in North Africa continue to face significant challenges, but also significant opportunities. We will continue to support them through these political and economic transitions. While we recognize that our budgets are facing increasing pressures, we are aligning our programs to address the challenges and opportunities facing the region. We also know that our continued engagement in this region is vital to maintaining relationships with key allies, promoting stability, countering extremist threats in the Middle East and North Africa and advancing our key strategic interests.

Chairman Kaine, Ranking Member Risch and distinguished members of the subcommittee, I appreciate the opportunity to appear before you today, and I look forward to answering your questions.

Senator KAINE. Great. I thank all of you for your opening testimony. To have the representatives of our defense, diplomacy, and development in the region is wonderful. It gives us a full view. And it is also, I think, particularly fitting, because AFRICOM, of our geographic commands, probably has the most integration of both military and the civilian governmental outreach in the African region. So it is fitting that you would all be here.

I want to begin with a question. You have each organized your comments largely around reports on the four countries individually, talking about the United States bilateral activities with respect to each.

Ms. Dory, you mentioned efforts to promote regional cooperation, and I would like each of you to address what is going on regionally, what do you do regionally that tries to link any or all of these four countries together, and possibly beginning with discussions of the current status of the Trans-Sahara Counterterrorism Partnership, which I know encompasses other nations as well. It is a 10-nation partnership.

But it does seem like there are some regional opportunities, so let us pick up on the regional cooperation theme. What is the current status? What can we do more to promote it?

Mr. SCHMIERER. Well, Mr. Chairman, let me start with a few general comments. As I think you indicated in your remarks, and I think all of us have underscored, the region as a whole is of great importance and has a lot to offer in terms of security and U.S. interests.

So one of our challenges has been to ensure, through our diplomatic and other engagement, that we can work with the governments of all four countries in ways that support each other. Clearly, as I was underscoring in my remarks, I think Morocco and Algeria present certain strengths which can be helpful to Libya and Tunisia.

So one of the issues—and I think my colleagues can address this more directly—is to try to use those strengths for security support throughout the region; likewise in terms of economic development. Unfortunately, it is a region in which there is not sufficient economic integration, and that drags down the economic prospects of the region.

And so one of our efforts—and again, through some of our other lines of activity—we are seeking to try to break down those barriers and encourage that kind of joint economic effort.

But the countries of the region do provide a lot of value. Morocco comes to mind. Morocco is the center of very moderate Islam. It is the center which is looked to throughout the region as a place to try to help moderate some of the extremists and to try to have that kind of influence broadly beyond its borders, and we try to work with them to leverage that both in the Maghreb and in the Sahel, particularly with Mali.

Senator KAINE. Other comments on the regional cooperation side, Ms. Romanowski?

Ms. ROMANOWSKI. Yes. One of the very specific things we are doing is also under the G8 umbrella, and it is specifically to have launched the Deauville Transition Fund where this is actually a multilateral partnership that is intended to provide the assistance that bolsters reform efforts across the Middle East and North Africa, but also spur some economic collaboration, coordination, and some economic growth.

Through this fund, the United States is helping to marshal the international resources to advance the economic reforms. The fund is actually administered by the World Bank and funds proposals crafted by the governments in partnerships with the international financial institutions. It primarily provides technical assistance to support these economic reforms and opportunities for trade. It tries to build institutions, design reform, and strengthen government policies.

So that is one very significant fund that is designed to actually bring the region together. It specifically is limited to countries in the partnership, which is Jordan, Tunisia, Egypt, Morocco, Yemen, and Libya.

Senator KAINE. Ms. Dory, could you talk a little bit about the Trans-Sahara Counterterrorism Partnership, the current status of efforts and how successful that regional effort has been?

Ms. DORY. Senator, I would be glad to. I wove it into the remarks because I thought it was important to emphasize the regional dynamics that are so critical when you are looking at transnational threats and transnational flows across borders.

One of the challenges we face as the U.S. Government is in terms of our implementation. We typically implement on a bilateral basis through our embassies. But TSCTP, I think, is important as a regional initiative that has been in place for close to a decade at this point that really seeks to have broader regional effects in the way that resources are aligned, whether they are USAID resources, DOD resources, or State Department resources. So I think we have had success on the U.S. Government side, aligning ourselves to consider regional effects.

The other side of the coin is how do our African partners present themselves. And when you look across the continent of Africa, regional institutions are at different stages of development in each part of the continent, and even the part that we are focused on today in North Africa, the Arab Maghreb Union, for example, is the relevant regional entity, and it is less institutionally developed than some of the other regional organizations. In West Africa, for example, ECOWAS has a very strong economic component to it, as well as security component to it.

So I think we continually look for opportunities to strengthen existing regional institutions, and then to work in regional ways when we can. A very concrete example for Department of Defense would be when we are working with governments to host military exercises and we seek to involve participants from multiple other countries beyond the actual host nation where the exercise would be conducted.

Senator KAINE. Thank you.

A couple of questions about Morocco for Ms. Romanowski, if I could start with you. You referenced a project that is going to be announced between the United States and Morocco in connection with the King's visit. Could you elaborate on that a little bit?

Ms. ROMANOWSKI. Yes. It is actually a 5-year newly revised strategic country development plan that we do and we try to do every 5 years where we actually focus on whether we need to shift our programming, our emphasis, and we work closely with the Moroccan Government. In this particular 5-year strategy that we will be announcing actually this afternoon, we are focusing on continuing to build strong civil society organizations so that they can participate in the political process.

We are also focusing on our continued support for education, improving the education system, because at this point there are significant issues related to early dropout and underachievement.

And then we are also in line with shifting a lot of our focus across the region is to focus on much more job development and job programs, and how do we actually help the young people in Morocco but across the region to have the skills, the job skills, the leadership skills to get jobs that are relevant to the private sector that is looking for employment.

Senator KAINE. Thank you.

Mr. Schmierer, if I could ask you to talk a little bit about—well, first, before I ask the question, the point that was made about Morocco that I find compelling is, along with Algeria, its capacity to be an example for the other nations, Tunisia and Libya. It is so much better to have an example that is near to home rather than to have to point out an example far away. Morocco's history of respect for religious minorities, some of the advances recently in opportunities for women in the commercial and civic spheres are very strong examples that I think we should be highlighting.

So a couple of questions, if you would. I know a continuing challenge, and I referenced it in my opening statement, has been the status of the western Sahara, and that is a challenge that is in the U.N. province now. It is a source of tension between Morocco and Algeria, and I am a little concerned about it especially because if porous borders are one of our challenges in the region, disputed territory suggests to me a potential vulnerability. I am sure it is an actual vulnerability as well.

It seems that the western Sahara situation has been in kind of a diplomatic stasis for some time. But could you talk about its current status and what U.S. policy is with respect to a resolution?

Mr. SCHMIERER. I would be happy to, and you are certainly correct to point out that this is a long-standing source of tension, and unfortunately tension among countries in the regional as well, in addition to the issue itself.

Our position is that we fully support the U.N. Secretary General's efforts, and we are very fortunate to have a very able diplomat, Ambassador Chris Ross, as his personal envoy to try to continue to resolve this issue, and he has been out there numerous times recently to talk to the various parties.

There have been some viable proposals made, and we certainly want to give those the opportunity to be looked at, and ultimately we think there should be, and could be, a peaceful, sustainable, and mutually agreed solution. But the parties will be the ones that will ultimately have to make that resolution.

So we continue to put our support behind the U.N. Secretary General and Ambassador Chris Ross to try to continue to move that issue forward.

Senator KAINE. Do you have any sense, Mr. Schmierer, of the timing or what you would foresee? I know it has been an open-ended issue for now, year after year.

Mr. SCHMIERER. It is 35 years, I think, is the time.

Senator KAINE. Yes.

Mr. SCHMIERER. So, yes, it is a long-standing issue. It would be hard to speculate, but one might hope that the current dynamics in the region, where there is change underway, and I think there is new thinking underway, that I think with Ambassador Ross' engagement and his diplomatic skills and the support of the international community, one could certainly hope that we would begin to see some new ways forward that might actually bring us to a resolution.

Senator KAINE. What is your assessment of the reform efforts undertaken by King Mohammed since the Arab Awakening began?

Mr. SCHMIERER. Well, of course, even when he first came to office in 1939, he began to make some reforms which I think were very well received, and certainly we were pleased and supportive of those reforms. That effort has continued, as I pointed out. Under their new constitution they have now had elections, they have an Islamist-led government, and we have seen a number of changes in the government leadership. So it is a dynamic governance situation, which I think has been very well received by the people.

At the same time, I also think that they are seeking more and more to bring in the kinds of values and principles that we have long since promoted. I think you referenced the fact that women and youth and various minorities now really do enjoy an improved situation and more opportunities.

So we just want to continue it, and I think the King's visit this week will give us that opportunity to continue to work with the Moroccans as they themselves seek to move further down the path that has been kind of opened up through the Arab Awakening.

Senator KAINE. And the accession to civilian political power of an Islamist-led government, it has not disturbed the relationship with the United States that has generally gone in that continuous way with the past history of good relations we have had?

Mr. SCHMIERER. Well, exactly. I think in the Moroccan context, one sees it a little bit differently than perhaps in some other contexts. But, no, absolutely. The fact that this resulted from their constitutional changes from a clearly understood to be free and fair election and that the government and the King have continued to work together, to us that has been a positive example of progressive change.

Senator KAINE. And then, Ms. Dory, one last question about Morocco. If you could just talk a little bit specifically about how the Moroccan military has been as a partner in dealing with the AQIM threat.

Ms. DORY. The Moroccan military, as I mentioned, we have had a very strong relationship over many years, and incorporated in the types of training activities that we do in terms of the exercises that we do, the focus on al-Qaeda and affiliates is central in the types of conversations and activities that are underway with the Moroccan military.

We have been very encouraged—even though Morocco is not a neighbor of Mali—with the events in Mali in the past 2 years, their concerns and considerations there and the work that they are doing to support the efforts. The AFISMA force that is in place, the multinational peace force, Moroccans have provided a field hospital to that effort, and they are in the process of providing training that will be religious training for imams who are based in Mali to help with the dimensions of countering violent extremism in Mali. So even well beyond their borders, Morocco has had a long history of participation in peacekeeping operations, and they continue to be quite engaged in the region.

The other thing I would flag is Moroccan leadership in hosting a border security ministerial in the last couple of weeks that was attended by its neighbors in North Africa, and again the demonstration of leadership well beyond its borders.

Senator KAINE. Thank you.

Let me ask a question, switching to Algeria for a minute, sort of make an observation. I may be right; I may be wrong; and tell me I am wrong, if I am wrong.

Algeria from outside review seems to have some challenges. So, for example, in youth unemployment and disaffected youth. And yet, it does also seem from outside review that they have not been beset with significant civil unrest. Is that correct? And if so, how do you interpret that? The absence of civil unrest is a notable thing in the region, and I would kind of like to get your opinions about that.

Mr. SCHMIERER. I would be happy to offer at least our reviews. Algeria, of course, is a country with considerable resources, and therefore a certain amount of wealth. Of course, it is the largest country in Africa, but it is a country whose resources are well matched with its population. So I think the government has tried to provide opportunities there for their large youth cohort.

We believe that more can be done in terms of free market development and those kinds of things. But I think to this point, the government has been fairly successful in directing its resources in ways that have supported the people, and as a result they have maintained a certain level of stability.

Senator KAINE. On the counterterrorism side, the Algerian military has had its own experience, sadly, but that has enabled them to be very battle-hardened and a pretty significant security partner.

Ms. Dory, you described that relationship a bit in your opening statement. But if you would talk a little bit about the capacities of the Algerian military, kind of along the lines of could they offer assistance to other nations, be they actual or kind of by example and by technical training, based on the experiences that they've had?

Ms. DORY. Senator, as you referenced, the Algerians have had a searing experience internally in dealing with AQIM and are a very fine counterterrorism force at this point. They have been working to focus on securing their borders in the past year and a half or so, with all of the events in Mali, and I think that is well known.

But what is less known, and we have encouraged them to speak more about it, is the support that they provide to some of their neighbors in the Sahel when it comes to training and equipment assistance. So in addition to being a strong counterterrorism operating force within their own borders, they are also sharing that expertise with other partners.

In terms of the relationship with the United States, I would say we have a growing relationship with the Algerians, particularly in recent times where we are having additional dialogues as it pertains to counterterrorism. We are sharing information. They are very interested, for example, in improvised explosive devices and some of the tactics, techniques, and procedures that the United States has developed in the course of operations in Afghanistan and Iraq. This is something within the Algerian context where AQIM activities, the kind of continued evolution on their part, there is a growing IED threat within Algeria that is forming the basis of some of the collaboration that we have at this point, both in terms of information-sharing as well as looking at equipment that we would be able to share with the Algerians.

Senator KAINE. Ms. Romanowski, maybe I am wrong on this. USAID does not currently have significant programs in Algeria; correct?

Ms. ROMANOWSKI. Chairman, that is correct. USAID has an extremely limited presence. We have been working to launch a program that is consistent with our combating terrorism and extremist programs, but that program we tend to do from Morocco where we do have a mission and have had one for a long time.

Senator KAINE. Is that status of only limited activity in Algeria likely to change in terms of USAID planning in the foreseeable future?

Ms. ROMANOWSKI. I do not see anything on the horizon that would allow us or enable us to change that, but when we have opportunities, particularly with respect to regional programs, we will take every opportunity we can.

Senator KAINE. Let me move to Tunisia, and this would be a question maybe for all of you to weigh in, if you care to, starting with Mr. Schmierer. Talk about the national dialogue, kind of the status of the national dialogue currently. Again, a number of things have gone well in Tunisia, but the two political assassinations this year obviously have led to significant unrest, some probably productive civil unrest. This is not the direction we want to go, but if you could talk about how that factors into the ongoing national dialogue?

Mr. SCHMIERER. Well, as you noted, Tunisia is the birthplace of the Arab Spring and now the ongoing Arab Awakening. So I think everybody is looking to try to help Tunisia get through what is turning out to be a difficult challenge. The two political assassinations of earlier this year have led to a call for a national dialogue and a transitional government.

The steps that are needed to be taken, first the parties need to select an independent figure to be the leader of the caretaker government, and right now the parties are regrouping to try to get to that point. Once that has been agreed to, then once the legislature approves that, then there will be—the legislature will seat a 9-member electoral monitoring board and then develop a new electoral law, and then set the date for new elections, and then adopt a new constitution. So those are the step-wise procedures that would happen through the national dialogue effort.

Senator KAINE. One other question. Each of these countries have their own peculiarities, and one in Tunisia that I find fascinating is the powerful nature of the trade union federation, the UGGT. If you could just kind of describe, as part of the national dialogue, the role that the trade union federation plays, and is it likely to continue to play that kind of role going forward or will that likely alter as the national dialogue goes forward?

Mr. SCHMIERER. Well, as you pointed out, it is a very strong institution in Tunisia, and it has been for some time. So clearly, all the parties involved will be ensuring that they work with, and coordinate with, the trade union Congress. It would be hard to predict. I would anticipate that will continue because it has been an institution of long standing, but there are dynamics at play where potentially you could see other centers of power emerge, because they are still kind of getting into that new period following the revolution. But I think one would anticipate a continued strong role by the trade union conference.

Senator KAINE. And then currently, Ms. Dory, talk a little bit about the role of the AQIM affiliates and other extremist groups like Ansar al-Sharia in Tunisia, if you could.

Ms. DORY. Tunisia immediately post-revolution has focused on the political process, as it needed to. But I think there has been the growing realization within Tunisia, in particular with Ansar al-Sharia, they took the step after a period of time of designating Ansar al-Sharia as a terrorist organization, recognizing that it was operating outside the boundaries of a political entity within their political process.

The Tunisian military has faced recent challenges in terms of attacks against the military in their positioning along the Algerian border and are in the process of undertaking a quite kinetic series of engagements against Ansar al-Sharia and other extremist organizations in their country. So I think that is something that we continue to need to be vigilant vis-a-vis the possibility that additional fighters flow into Tunisia or through Tunisia given the challenges associated with the borders with Libya and with Mali.

Senator KAINE. Overshadowed by the Benghazi attack was the fact that the Embassy in Tunis was also attacked within a few days thereafter, thank goodness not in such a serious way, and that is one of the reasons it was overshadowed. But have we done what we need to do, learned the lessons from that attack as well, and provided additional security as needed to our diplomatic personnel in Tunisia, Mr. Schmierer?

Mr. SCHMIERER. I would say very strongly, "Yes." As I am sure you are aware, our top priority is the security of our people, of our facilities, and of Americans abroad. And as you suggest, that was a very unfortunate incident but one which has caused us to redouble our assessments and our efforts in terms of security. I know Ambassador Wallace has been very active on both the physical security and on procedural measures to ensure that our Embassy in Tunisia is secure and has what it needs to ensure its security.

Senator KAINE. With respect, one last question on Tunisia before a few questions about Libya. It does appear that the United States has a very comprehensive approach to Tunisia from security assistance, economic assistance, a Millennium Challenge Corporation Threshold Program, and potential support for an eventual free trade agreement.

Are we getting good cooperation from other international partners in trying to devote this comprehensive approach to increasing stability and then eventually prosperity in Tunisia?

Mr. SCHMIERER. On the political front, absolutely. We are in very close contact with allies and with other countries in the region that also share our goals of stabilizing and helping Tunisia move forward, and that is true across the region, of all these transitioning countries. And so that is one really, I think, great success story, is a common commitment on the part of us and like-minded nations, whether they are Arab nations, European nations or others, to support these countries, and particularly Tunisia, in making a successful transition.

Senator KAINE. Moving to a few questions about Libya before moving on to the second panel.

Ms. Dory, you testified a little bit about the destruction of chemical weapons, and I do not want that to be lost for all the significant challenges that remain. The destruction of chemical weapons stockpiles is something that is very important to note and to praise our efforts in that. Did you indicate a date on which we believe the Libyan stockpile will be completely eliminated?

Ms. DORY. The current projection is by the end of the year.

Senator KAINE. And can you describe sort of the volume of the chemical weapons stockpile that we have been dealing with in trying to do that destruction?

Ms. DORY. I can. We have been working to destroy in the first instance a series of munitions that included artillery shells, hundreds of artillery shells, bombs and other munition cartridges, so a significant stockpile of munitions, and then there are other materials that will need to be destroyed as well from production of those munitions.

Senator KAINE. If we could, let us talk about the militias. I mean, some have called for an international effort, an international peacekeeping force to try to begin an engagement surrounding a massive disarmament effort among the militias. Is that a realistic proposal? Or describe whether that is a good idea and what we should be doing to advance it if it is a good idea.

Mr. SCHMIERER. That is not the approach that we are supporting. As I mentioned, we, and right now Italy and the United Kingdom, are all committed to helping stand up this general purpose force, and obviously our DOD colleagues will be the essential implementers on that, as the means of helping Libya establish the internal security which is currently not there. So we think that is an appropriate and ultimately will be the successful way to address the internal security issues in Libya.

Senator KAINE. And, Mr. Schmierer, you indicated that that training of that general purpose force would be at about—to the level of about 5,000 people that would be trained?

Mr. SCHMIERER. Yes. Our commitment coming out of the G8 was 5,000 to 8,000, and since that time the Italians and the British have also indicated, I believe, a commitment of 2,000 each. So those numbers will then be somewhere between 5,000 and 10,000. The Libyan Government is the sponsor and the funder of this effort, but obviously with our cooperation we would certainly be coming to the Congress for their input and their support for that effort.

Senator KAINE. And is that general purpose force, the size of it, is that to be sort of a core and it would ultimately be a much larger force, or how would that advance Libya toward its ultimate goal of having a significant and appropriately sized security apparatus?

Mr. SCHMIERER. I might have to defer to my DOD colleagues on force levels. It would be between 5,000 and 10,000. We would very well train the general purpose force for a country of 6 million. So I think ultimately that would really just be a good first start, as then they would institutionalize and go forward, a ''train the trainers'' kind of an effort.

Senator KAINE. What is the current status of functioning local governments in Libya, local elections, local governments, and is that a positive to the national government or is it seen at all as sort of a threat or competition?

Mr. SCHMIERER. Well, it is kind of a combination because at the local level you do have functioning communities. So you have local governments which are delivering services and which are operating in support of the people. Unfortunately, at the same time you also have security situations, militias and other instability. So that is not preventing local governments from doing the basic work that they would be doing, but ultimately that is not an effective way for them to continue functioning.

So, yes, I think one can say that basically those governments are functioning, but it is very important to get the security part fixed so that that can continue in a positive way.

Senator KAINE. Obviously, our involvement with NATO in Libya, we have continued to have international partners, for example, in training the general purpose force that you indicate. Is the United States satisfied with the degree of international participation across the range of the activities that we are currently engaged in in Libya? Are there enough partners at the table to help us make a difference?

Mr. SCHMIERER. I can certainly indicate the planning for the general purpose force, absolutely. And then also as we have looked at other elements of their capacity-building on the governance side, we have very strong commitments from a number of other allies to try to help Libyans stand up that civilian side, so to speak, of what needs to be developed in the country. So, yes, I think the international community has done a very good job both of standing up and of coordinating their support.

Senator KAINE. Could you talk a little bit about the governance initiatives and what is currently under way?

Mr. SCHMIERER. Well, there are a number of planning processes where the idea would be to try to help—what they are lacking now is the ability to actually execute the functions of government. So they have resources, but they really do not even have good budgetary execution capability. So having the resources has not allowed them to actually address the kinds of issues that they face.

So we have not launched anything at this point, but we are working with the Libyans and with allies and friends to try to conceptualize and then develop and launch an effort to identify and help the Libyans stand up the capacities that they need to use their resources effectively to address the governance challenges that they face.

Senator KAINE. I want to say that is sufficient questions for Panel 1. Senator Risch came in and I offered him the chance to make opening statements, and I said please ask questions, and he said to me that normally we are hemmed in by 5- or 6-minute question rounds, and he said he was going to cede me time to ask as many as I wanted. So it has been good to have the chance to dialogue with you for about an hour. I appreciate the testimony and the efforts to address these concerns of the first panel, and thank you very much for participating.

I would like to ask the second panel now to come on up.

Thank you.

[Pause.]

Senator KAINE. Well, I would like to welcome the second panel before us. I will do brief introductions of the panel members and then ask them to testify in the order in which I introduce them.

Dr. William Lawrence is currently a visiting professor of political science and international affairs at George Washington, at the Elliott School of International Affairs there. From 2011 to 2013, he was director of the North Africa Project at the International Crisis Group, and prior to that served in a number of positions in the U.S. State Department, including service at the U.S. Embassy in Tripoli. Dr. Lawrence spent 12 years in North Africa, and he served with the late Ambassador Chris Stevens in the Peace Corps in Morocco.

Frederic Wehrey is a senior associate in the Middle East Program at the Carnegie Endowment for International Peace. His research has focused on political reform and security issues in the Arab Gulf States and U.S. policy in the Middle East more broadly. He flew back from Libya just yesterday.

Thank you for accepting our invite when you are so jet-lagged, where you have been studying and working on the various Libya militias. Obviously, we look forward to hearing about your most recent experience.

Thomas Joscelyn, our third witness, is a senior fellow at the Foundation for Defense of Democracies, and also senior editor of the Long War Journal, a publication dealing with counterterrorism and related security issues. Much of his research focuses on how al-Qaida and its affiliates operate around the globe. Mr. Joscelyn was the senior counterterrorism advisor to Mayor Giuliani during his 2008 Presidential campaign and has testified often before Congress.

If I could begin with Dr. Lawrence and have each of you do opening statements, we will get into questions. We are expecting votes to be called sometime between 3:45 and 4:00, and we will engage in vigorous questioning until we have to run over to the floor.

But, Dr. Lawrence, welcome, and please begin.

STATEMENT OF WILLIAM LAWRENCE, VISITING PROFESSOR OF POLITICAL SCIENCE AND INTERNATIONAL AFFAIRS, GEORGE WASHINGTON UNIVERSITY'S ELLIOTT SCHOOL OF INTERNATIONAL AFFAIRS, WASHINGTON, DC

Dr. LAWRENCE. Thank you, Chairman Kaine, and thank you to all those who helped organize the panel. As you mentioned, I just spent 2 years in the region witnessing all this from up close, and although I will only be able to cover so much in 5 minutes, I am happy to answer any questions you have about the individual countries, and any questions you asked the first panel insofar as it does not get into the nitty-gritty of U.S. programs. I would be happy to address any of those questions.

In the North African region and beyond, we are still living in what historians call a "world historical moment" where change happens fast in profound but cacophonous ways. History accelerates, and we often miss much of what is going on and get distracted by things over here and miss what is going on over there.

Apt comparisons have been made to 1989 in Eastern Europe and to 1945, but I think the best comparison is to 1848, in which the authoritarians play themselves, the liberals play themselves, the street plays itself, and the Marxist spoilers are replaced by Islamist spoilers. And even though only one country had a regime change in 1848, about 20 countries in Europe were profoundly affected, and this began a process of the decline of monarchies and the growth of democracies in Europe.

Of the 18 countries that rose up in the winter of 2011, the North African nations played a much larger role than the nations to the east. They incubated this change over quite a long period. They provided much of the political culture, the slogans, the rap lyrics, the hybridic ideologies, and North Africa continues to be the place where most of the change is taking place in the Arab Spring's aftermath.

In a lecture I gave 2 years ago in Boston entitled "Days of Rage, Dreams of Trespass," you can hear a lot of this analysis that I am talking about. But suffice it to say that today the roots of rage and the dreams of trespass have not subsided in this region, and we cannot rely on the media. The media is too underfunded and underresourced, and it is not everywhere.

Just take the example of Bloody Friday last Friday in Tripoli where we had a massacre of civilians and a civilian uprising against militias and very poor media coverage, and this could be a major turning point in the politics of Libya and the politics of Tripoli. This civilian uprising was much like the civilian uprising after Chris Stevens' death in Benghazi, and yet it gets lost in this environment of big change.

That also raises an important quick point I will make about Libya, which is that Libya is not one big mess. Libya is a bunch of little messes that are not very related. So the string of political assassinations in Benghazi is very different from the political game involving militias and their GNC allies in Tripoli, which is different from what is going on in the borders, which is different from the fighting over smuggling and trafficking routes in the south, and different from ethnic conflicts in other communities, and we tend to conflate this all because there is no military and no police, and we do a great disservice to ourselves to not understand all the different dynamics in these different Libyan localities.

Over the last 3 years and across the North African region, we are talking about major changes every month with national, regional, and global causes and effects, and we do ourselves a disservice by focusing on nation/state-level changes and ignoring the subnational and the transnational.

There are also dozens of ways the information coming from the region gets distorted as it flows through various filters coming to Washington. One of the big ones I call the Egypt Effect. When Egypt is going well, the region is going well; and when Egypt is doing badly, everyone else is suffering from whatever malady Egypt has, whereas Tunisia in particular is very much on its own trajectory and should not be viewed through that Egyptian lens.

That said, there are regional dimensions to all this, and what we often miss is what is regional. For example, I would venture to say that Egypt is not the big problem in North Africa right now. Syria is the big problem. We have thousands of fighters streaming to Syria. We have hundreds of deaths already of North Africans in Syria, and we have blowback effects already starting, not unlike the young fighters coming back from Afghanistan that had a direct impact on the 1990s happening in Algeria.

So we do ourselves a great disservice by not understanding that by putting the Syria conflict on hold, it does not constrain itself. It rocks the North African region in very profound ways. Take, for example, the flows of jihadists and the flows of weapons, right? We were mostly concerned in 2011 about flows to the west and to the south. Now that is not the concern. It is the flows back into Libya because Libyan militias over-sold into the black markets, and the increasing flows north and east of Libya toward the conflicts that you mentioned.

It is also not correct to see the change that happened in North Africa as nonviolent. And it is also incorrect to see stability as needing to be our number one goal in the region. Stability for stability's sake, as we have learned, has destabilizing effects in the region. Democratic transitions are unstable. Three hundred Tunisians died in their revolution. Twenty-seven thousand Libyans died in their revolution, and the vast majority of the deaths were pro-revolution Libyans fighting and now continuing that fight in Syria, as I mentioned earlier, because they want change in their countries.

The other martyrs often get overlooked. Bouazizi was the first of 400 self-immolations across the region, the majority in Algeria, and the majority of these self-immolators worked in the informal sector, and the international community and the national communities have continued the same economic policies toward the informal sectors, which do not work. So we continue to exclude from the formal economies, because not enough jobs are being created, and from the informal economies, and have this continuing cycle. Even this month, we have had several new self-immolations because of the despair.

Fifty percent of the people in all of these countries work in the informal sector. Thirty percent of the economies, on average, are in the informal sector. And we are not doing a good job in terms of job creation and making the informal sector into an engine of growth rather than a problem that needs to be eradicated.

North African young people made these revolutions, and they continue to be successful in keeping change happening. But we also should not see them as those kids over there. In many ways, it was our investments in vaccinations, our investments in mother-child health care, our investments in education, our investments in any number of areas that created the youth bulge in the first place, which is not created by high fertility. It is created by mortality dropping twice as quickly as fertility is dropping in the region, and many of these kids, many of the revolutionaries studied in American universities. They were our classmates, they were our students, and as things continue to unfold, they are wondering why we are not there more.

So in many ways, the chickens of successful developmental policy, both domestic and international, have come home to roost, and we have not sufficiently adjusted our assistance policies to take into account these new realities, where big investments in health and education and women and youth on the old models create as many problems, as I mentioned earlier, as they solve, where the real action right now is the 10 million jobs that need to be created for this youth bulge that largesse and good will created in the first place.

I have interviewed over 5,000 young people in the region over many years, and if I have learned anything from these interviews, these are very pragmatic young people who have rejected the old ideologies, nationalist ideologies, socialist ideologies, Amazerist ideologies, feminist ideologies, Islamist ideologies, and the vast majority are seeking to build reconciled political spaces where everyone has a seat at the metaphorical dinner table.

I remember when youth activists from Abdul Asan, a banned Islamic group in Morocco, were crushed when their group left the February 20th movement because they wanted to build a Morocco where everyone had a seat at that table, where everyone worked together.

So we have restive populations with higher expectations because of the Arab Spring, and states, to quote Yahia Zoubir in his new book on security in the region, which are managers of violence. To whatever degree these states are to blame for that violence or are simply victims of that violence varies from state to state. But there is no question that all four states need help quelling the increased violence, some of it in the name of democratization and rights, some in the name of jobs and keeping price subsidies, and some of the more nefarious forces that we have been talking about.

But let us not get on the wrong side of democratic change, as we did in some of the cases in the Arab Spring, and always ask in our assistance and in our partnerships how does this policy affect the young people that are trying to emulate our system with their efforts to make political change? As we engage with the governments, we do not often think that way.

In security, and I was one of the people who worked on TSCTP when I was at the State Department, the creation of it, it was a good idea. It has not been fully implemented in as holistic a manner as it could have. We need to do a lot more in human rights, as the head of AFRICOM said and his regret in terms of what was done in Mali. We also need to do a lot more on the economic side and the political reform side.

Senator KAINE. If I could ask you to start to summarize, Dr. Lawrence.

Dr. LAWRENCE. I am right at the end.

So we need to increase levels of cooperation with all of these countries.

I am very concerned about our very light footprint in Libya and the tiny Embassy, and even our light footprint in Tunisia and Algeria where diplomats, because of what happened in Benghazi, are very much hunkered down. They do get out with their escorts, but they are very few in number. We do not have enough out there, and we need to get more out to the embassies, in my opinion.

I am optimistic for the long term in the Maghreb even though my prediction for the medium term is more mixed. The Maghreb needs our help, our heart and soft power, and our smart power.

Thank you.

Senator KAINE. Thank you, Dr. Lawrence.

Dr. Wehrey.

STATEMENT OF FREDERIC WEHREY, SENIOR ASSOCIATE IN THE MIDDLE EAST PROGRAM, CARNEGIE ENDOWMENT FOR INTERNATIONAL PEACE, WASHINGTON, DC

Dr. WEHREY. Good afternoon, Chairman Kaine. Thank you for the opportunity to speak about Libya's worsening security crisis and the next steps for United States policy in building Libya's Army.

I join you today having flown back last night from a 2-week trip to Tripoli and Benghazi, where I met with a wide range of Libyans, including militia leaders, military officers, parliamentarians, tribal chiefs, and Islamists about options to improve security.

These voices were nearly unanimous in identifying the unifying thread of much of Libya's instability in many of these disparate conflicts to the power and autonomy of the country's roughly 300 militias, many of which the Libyan Government has tried to bring under its control by putting them on its payroll. Now, by all accounts, this has been a disastrous bargain. It has actually given predatory militias even greater freedom and even greater latitude.

This past weekend, I witnessed a remarkable turn of events in Tripoli that suggests public patience with the militias has reached a tipping point. On Friday, peaceful protesters marched on a compound belonging to a powerful militia from Misrata, demanding that they leave. Forty-six of these protesters died at the hands of militiamen wielding heavy-caliber weapons. The outrage was immediate. Civil strikes shut down the city, and protests erupted across Libya.

The message in all of this activism was uniform and clear: We want the militias dismantled, and we want the legitimate army and police to take their place.

Now, echoing these popular demands, the United States, as we have heard, along with Italy and Britain, is considering a plan to train and equip a new Libyan national army, denoted in military terms as a general purpose force. In theory, the concept is sound: bolster the army to protect the elected officials and institutions and compel the militias to disarm.

But the plan also carries several risks. Unanswered questions about the force's mission, its oversight, and its inclusiveness could further polarize an already-fractured country. To prevent this from happening, the following five issues and questions regarding the general purpose force need to be resolved.

First, its exact role and mission needs to be clarified, and based on my last visit, it is not clear that the Libyans have the capacity to determine this at this point. As its name implies, it is meant to be a conventional infantry force that is focused on guarding installations and officials, but what Libya really needs is a more specialized gendarme to tackle border security, illicit trafficking in narcotics and weapons, and low-level insurgency.

Second, effective civilian oversight of this force must be in place. Libya does not need to follow an all-too-common model in the Arab world where armies' self-entitlement and insularity have been fatal for democracy. The Libyan revolution was not launched to replace one colonel with another.

Third, the general purpose force must act and be perceived as nonpartisan and professional. To prevent it from becoming the private militia of a particular tribe or region, or the Pretorian Guard for a political faction, its recruits must draw from a broad spectrum of Libyan society and must be integrated into mixed units.

Fourth, the United States and Libyan authorities must properly vet recruits for aptitude, human rights' violations, and criminal history. Recent failures bear this out. An effort last year to train Libyan police officers in Jordan collapsed when poorly screened recruits mutinied against what they perceived as poor conditions.

Fifth and perhaps most important, the training effort must be accompanied by a parallel program to demobilize and reintegrate the young men in the militias back into society. These young men must be given economic and social incentives to leave and enter the workforce, pursue schooling, or join the regular police and army. Doing so would deprive militia bosses and cynical politicians of the manpower to obstruct Libya's democratic transition.

Mr. Chairman, in light of the stunning display of public activism and government will that I witnessed this weekend, the United States and Libya's friends have a window of opportunity to help improve Libya's security. But the United States needs to proceed cautiously and deliberately. True, establishing an army is an important first step in restoring security. But the militia problem cannot be solved solely by the state's monopolization of force.

The militias draw from a wellspring of deep political and economic grievances by Libya's long-neglected towns and regions, and better training and equipment alone will not confer legitimacy on the new army or compel militias to surrender their arms. That legitimacy will only be obtained through broad political reconciliation such as the national dialogue currently being sponsored by the Prime Minister, a constitution, and a representative government that is able to deliver services across the country.

Thank you for the opportunity to speak here today.

[The prepared statement of Dr. Wehrey follows:]

PREPARED STATEMENT OF DR. FREDERIC WEHREY

Chairman Kaine, Ranking Member Risch, committee members, I am grateful for this opportunity to speak with you about Libya's worsening security crisis and the next steps for U.S. policy in building Libya's Army.

I join you today having flown back last night from a 2-week research trip to Tripoli, western mountains and the troubled eastern city of Benghazi. It was my sixth visit to the country and my fourth since the Revolution.

The focus of my recent trip was to assess the prospects for demobilizing and disarming the country's powerful militias while building up the regular army and police and reforming its defense institutions. I held frank and detailed conversations with a variety of official and nonofficial actors: the Special Forces commander in charge of securing Benghazi, militant federalists in the east, the heads of Islamist militias, civil society activists, and parliamentarians.

DIAGNOSING THE PROBLEM

Much of Libya's worsening crisis stems from the power and autonomy of the country's roughly 300 militias. Lacking its own police and army, the transitional government in late 2011 and 2012, cut a deal with these militias, putting them on the payroll of the Ministries of Defense and Interior. By all accounts this has been a Faustian bargain that has given the militias freedom to pursue agendas that are political, ideological, in some cases, purely criminal.

The militia menace has been especially stark in Tripoli, where armed groups from outside the city—Misrata and Zintan—have claimed what they see as the spoils of the revolution, occupying public and governmental institutions, raiding the army's training camps and facilities, and pressuring the Parliament to pass legislation. In the east, militias allied with the country's federalists have shut down oil production while in the south they guard the porous frontier.

Over the weekend, I witnessed a remarkable turn of events in Tripoli that suggest public patience with the militias has reached a tipping point. On Friday protestors marched peacefully on a compound in Tripoli belonging to a powerful, predatory Misratan militia, demanding that they leave. Forty-six people, including the elderly, women, and several adolescents, died in a hail of gunfire by militiamen wielding heavy caliber weapons. The message was uniform and clear: "We want the militias out of Tripoli, and the national army and police to take their place."

When I left Tripoli, the Libyan national police and army—long thought to be nonexistent and missing in action—were out on the streets of Tripoli in full force, to thunderous applause from the city's residents. The question before us now is whether this remarkable episode presages a real dismantlement of militia power, or whether it is simply a tactical redeployment.

U.S. SECURITY ASSISTANCE: OPPORTUNITIES AND CHALLENGES

In response to Libyan's deepening crisis and Prime Minister Zeidan's request for greater outside assistance at this year's G8, the U.S., Italy, Britain, and Turkey are planning to train and equip a new Libyan national army, denoted in military terms as a "general purpose force." In theory, the concept seems sound: bolster a professional Libyan Army to protect elected officials and institutions, allow the government to function free from militia pressure, and compel the militias to disarm.

But the plan also carries the risks. Unanswered questions about the force's oversight, mission, inclusiveness of different regions, and composition could potentially polarize and destabilize Libya's already tenuous landscape. Many Islamists in the east believe the planned army is hardly a national one but rather a palace guard for the Prime Minister. Already there are signs that militias are trying to bloody the nose of the new army before it even gets off the ground.

To avoid potential pitfalls, the following issues and questions need to be resolved:

First, the exact role of the general purpose force needs to be determined. As its name implies, it is meant to be a regular infantry, focused initially on securing government installations and protecting officials. But what Libya really needs is a more specialized, gendarmerie-type service to tackle border security, illicit trafficking in narcotics and weapons, and low-level insurgency.

It does not need another bloated, conventional military force that sits in its barracks—a far too common occurrence in the Arab world, where armies' self-entitlement and insularity have proved unhealthy for democracy. The Libyan revolution was not launched to replace one colonel for another.

Second, the "general purpose" force must be, and must be perceived as, nonpartisan and professional. To prevent it from becoming a private militia of a particular tribe, region, or political clique, recruits must be integrated into mixed units that draw from a broad swath of Libyan society. The case of a separate and under-reported U.S. effort to train a small Libyan counterterrorism unit inside Libya earlier this year is instructive. The unit, set up by U.S. special operations forces, was hardly representative of Libya's regional makeup: recruitment appeared to be drawn overwhelmingly from westerners to the exclusion of the long-neglected east.

And at least some of the new enlisted ranks and junior officer corps must come from the militias. Many senior officers in the Libyan Army detest that idea, viewing the militiamen as ill-disciplined rabble or excessively politicized. In many cases, though, these young men bring the real-world battlefield experience and small unit leadership that is so desperately needed in the Libyan Army, whose junior and mid-level officer ranks Qaddafi had hollowed out.

Teaching recruits to function as cohesive fighting units—rather than focusing solely on imparting individual soldiering skills—is also essential. The training mission cannot just produce soldiers who are better marksmen but who return to Libya and melt into the militias, or who moonlight as militiamen in addition to their day job in the army. To prevent that worst-case scenario, proper vetting for motivation, aptitude, past human rights violations, and criminal history is also vital. Recent failures bear this out: an effort last year to train Libyan police officers in Jordan collapsed when poorly screened recruits mutinied against what they perceived as unduly Spartan living conditions.

Third, and perhaps most important, the training program must be accompanied by a reinvigorated demobilization, disarmament, and reintegration program for those in the militias. These young men must be given economic and social incentives to leave and either enter the work force, pursue schooling, or join the regular police and army. Many of the revolutionary fighters I have spoken with over the past 2 years do not want to remain in the militias. But few real alternatives exist.

Mr. Chairman, to conclude: given the stunning display of popular and government willpower I witnessed this weekend, the U.S. and Libya's friends face an important window of opportunity to help improve Libya's security situation. But the U.S. needs to proceed cautiously and deliberately. Better training and equipment alone will not automatically confer legitimacy on the new army, compel militias to surrender their arms, or entice Libyans to join up.

That legitimacy will only be obtained through broad political reconciliation, a constitution, and a representative government that is able to deliver services across the country.

In this respect, U.S. security policy must take a holistic view. It must go beyond building an army to include sustained assistance to the Prime Minister's ongoing initiative of National Dialogue that can establish agreed upon "rules of the game" and address and mitigate the deep seated roots of the political disenchantment that fuels the militias' persistence. The U.S. must also lend advice and expertise to the ongoing constitutional process that will ensure proper civilian control of the military and delineate authorities between federal and municipal government.

Senator KAINE. Thank you, Dr. Wehrey.
Mr. Joscelyn.

STATEMENT OF THOMAS JOSCELYN, SENIOR FELLOW, FOUNDATION FOR DEFENSE OF DEMOCRACIES, WASHINGTON, DC

Mr. JOSCELYN. Chairman Kaine, thank you very much for having me here to talk about the threat environment in North Africa. Just by way of quick background, I come from this a little bit different perspective as I am basically a nerd who studies al-Qaeda very carefully and granularly. So I am going to talk a little bit about— in the first panel we heard about what we are doing in North Africa. I want to talk a little bit about what our enemies are doing.

Senator KAINE. Good, good.

Mr. JOSCELYN. And I am going to tailor my comments. I am going to scratch what I was going to talk about and basically just talk about some of the issues that you raised in the first panel.

The first one is, you raised the issue of what we are doing regionally as opposed to the bilateral agreements with individual countries. I think that is exactly the right way to think about it. Our enemies are organized regionally. In fact, Al Qaeda in the Islamic Maghreb is the regional emirate of a global terrorist network. That is how it is set up. It is basically set up to set up an Islamic state.

This is seen throughout much of its history as a pipedream. They have had very little success until, really, its takeover of two-thirds of Mali. However, we have seen AQIM has really accelerated its operations in a variety of ways. Dr. Lawrence talked about the network effects to Syria and elsewhere throughout the Middle East, and that is exactly right. Basically, this is not just a security problem for North Africa but it affects things throughout the region and even globally.

In October, in fact, the State Department and then the U.N. designated a top Egyptian terrorist named Muhammed Jamal al-Khashef, who was reporting directly to Ayman al-Zawahiri. He was directly in communication with him. Some of his trainees actually took part in the Benghazi terrorist attack last year.

Jamal is a good example of how this network effect works, because he is working with both Al Qaeda in the Islamic Maghreb, Al Qaeda in the Arabian Peninsula. He established his own training camps in the Sinai, eastern Libya, and was even dispatching fighters to Mali. So that is one of many examples I can give you about how this sort of works as a network regionally.

The second thing I want to talk about, obviously al-Qaeda is just part of the picture. There is a broad spectrum of issues here which the other witnesses can better speak to than I can. However, one of the things I would like to talk about is that we continually underestimate, I think, what al-Qaeda's clandestine plans are for various regions. We have seen this in Iraq, we saw this in Yemen, and we have seen this in Syria, where al-Qaeda's two affiliates have taken over a large portion of territory.

AQIM now, having taken over Mali, they have been kicked out by the French, showed that it had the capacity to do more than just smuggling and contraband and kidnappings for ransom, that sort of thing.

To that effect, in early October a top alleged al-Qaeda operative named Abu al-Salibi was captured by U.S. forces in Tripoli. What's interesting is that most of the press coverage focused on his historical acts on behalf of al-Qaeda, including his involvement in the 1998 Embassy bombings, which I think is well established in the court record.

What I was more interested in is what a report prepared by the Library of Congress in conjunction with an arm of the Defense Department concluded about Abu al-Salibi's role, all the way back in August 2012. They concluded, the authors of that report, that, in fact, he was the clandestine builder of al-Qaeda's network in Libya in the wake of the revolution, and that he had a series of steps that he was following under guidance from al-Qaeda's senior leadership to build up al-Qaeda's presence in Libya, including working with various militias and sort of ingraining al-Qaeda's ideology locally within Libya.

And that brings me to the third point. There is oftentimes a distinction that has been made, I think a false one, that al-Qaeda is sort of this global jihadist threat and it is not really connected to these local endeavors, it is not really a local jihadist organization as well. That is fundamentally wrong. In fact, al-Qaeda, throughout its entire existence, has spent most of its resources, overwhelmingly so, on local endeavors, and what we are seeing now in Tunisia or Libya and elsewhere is really how it is actually moving forward with those designs.

And you raised the issue of Ansar al-Sharia of Tunisia and its attack, or you also mentioned the two assassinations earlier this year, and also the attack on our U.S. Embassy. Well, the Tunisia Government has blamed Ansar al-Sharia of Tunisia for all of that. They say that Ansar al-Sharia of Tunisia was actually responsible for the political assassinations, and the State Department has recognized that they were responsible for the attack on our Embassy. They actually are strong ties between that branch of Ansar al-Sharia and also the Ansar al-Sharia in Libya.

The reason why I connect the dots on this a little bit is that Ansar al-Sharia in Tunisia—you can see it in my written testimony, and I can go on with a lot more evidence—I think is firmly part of the al-Qaeda network inside North Africa, as is Ansar al-Sharia in Libya, and there is a lot of data on that that I have been compiling. These are groups I follow every day online. These are groups that I have been tracking very closely.

Why is that important? Well, it shows al-Qaeda's designs and the al-Qaeda network's designs do have local interests, and this raises the whole point that you were getting at in terms of our partnerships with these various countries. Part of the thing that we have to emphasize here is that our interests are very much the same as Tunisia's in combating these terrorists in the al-Qaeda network, as in Libya and elsewhere, where these local interests that al-Qaeda has, they also can manifest themselves against us. There is also a threat to us from them, as we saw with the attack on the U.S. Embassy in Tunis just 3 days after the attack in Benghazi.

And I will just leave it there. Thanks.

[The prepared statement of Mr. Joscelyn follows:]

PREPARED STATEMENT OF THOMAS JOSCELYN

Chairman Kaine, Ranking Member Risch, and members of the committee, thank you for inviting me here today to discuss the security situation in North Africa. For more than a decade I have been closely tracking al-Qaeda and associated movements. So, my testimony today will largely focus on the al-Qaeda network in North and West Africa and how this network has evolved over time.

The Arab uprisings that began in late 2010 and early 2011 created new opportunities for millions of oppressed people. Unfortunately, the overthrow of several dictators also generated new space for al-Qaeda and like-minded organizations to operate. How the political process will play out in any of these nations in the coming decades is extremely difficult, if not impossible, for any prognosticator to say. But we do know this: The Arab revolutions not been the death knell for al-Qaeda as some analysts claimed it would be.

Instead, al-Qaeda and other ideologically allied organizations have taken advantage of the security vacuums caused by the uprisings. In Mali, for instance, an al-Qaeda branch that was once written off as nothing more than a ''nuisance'' to the residents of the countries in which it operated managed to take over a large swath of territory, thereby forcing the French to intervene.[1] Al Qaeda in the Islamic Maghreb (AQIM) and its allies imposed their harsh sharia law on the residents of Mali at gunpoint, destroying local Muslim traditions and practices until the jihadists could be dislodged from power. Even now, however, the al-Qaeda-led alliance threatens Mali. Many of the jihadist fighters melted away into neighboring countries, where, free from the West's superior military might, they have regrouped and lived to fight another day.[2]

Al-Qaeda did not overthrow the government in Mali, but, as was the case elsewhere, the international terror network took advantage of the situation. A coup d'etat by Malian soldiers unseated the elected government and set in motion a chain of events that AQIM capitalized on. Armed with weapons formerly kept in Col. Muammar al-Qaddafi's arsenals, al-Qaeda, other jihadist groups and Tuareg tribesmen quickly ran roughshod over the Malian military.

The war in Mali is instructive because it shows how events throughout the region, including inside the countries we were asked to assess today, are interconnected. Qaddafi's weapons fueled the fight in Mali, but post-Qaddafi Libya's instability and porous borders have escalated the violence as well. Fighters who took part in the Libyan revolution returned to Mali with fresh combat experience. Al-Qaeda and allied jihadists have established training camps inside Libya and newly trained fighters have been able to move across Algeria into Mali.

The threat of terrorism inside Algeria has increased during the war in Mali. In January 2013, an al-Qaeda commander named Mokhtar Belmokhtar laid siege to the In Amenas gas facility. Belmokhtar's forces have fought in Mali and operated inside Libya as well. Algerian authorities claim that some of the Egyptians who took part in the In Amenas operation also participated in the September 11, 2012, terrorist attack in Benghazi, Libya. Tunisian authorities have blamed veterans from Mali with links to AQIM for security problems along the border with Algeria.[3]

The war in Mali is tied, therefore, to broader regional security problems that stretch into and throughout all of North Africa. In fact, the terrorist threats in North Africa are tied to events that occur even farther away—in Syria, for example. Al Qaeda in Iraq drew many recruits from North Africa during the height of the Iraq war. With the Syrian war raging on, al-Qaeda's two affiliates in Syria continue to draw fighters from North Africa's jihadist pool. These same fighters can pose threats to their home countries upon their return.

KEY POINTS

This brief introduction is a way of saying that the terrorist threat emanating from North and West Africa is a dynamic problem set with no easy solutions. Still, the last several years have revealed to us certain key lessons. Any sound strategy for defeating al-Qaeda and its allies should take the following into account:

- AQIM leads a network that operates in several countries. This network is comprised of not just individuals and brigades that are formally a part of AQIM, but also entities that are closely allied with the al-Qaeda branch. If we are to defeat the AQIM network, then the West and its local allies must understand AQIM's order of battle—that is, how all of these groups are operating in conjunction with one another. There are differences between some of these groups, but at the end of the day they are in the same trench. I discuss this further below.
- The AQIM network includes groups that are frequently identified as "local" jihadist organizations. It is widely believed that groups such as Ansar al-Dine and the Ansar al-Sharia chapters are not really a part of the al-Qaeda network in North and West Africa. But, as I explain, this view is based on a fundamental misreading of al-Qaeda's objectives.
- Western analysts should be careful not to underestimate the current or future capabilities of al-Qaeda's many branches. Prior to its takeover of much of Mali, the AQIM threat was widely viewed as a criminal problem. Kidnappings for ransom, contraband smuggling, and extortion were and remain key AQIM operations. But the organization and its allies have now demonstrated a much more lethal capability. They have proven capable of taking and holding territory in the absence of effective central government control. Given that some of the governments in North Africa have only a tenuous grip on power, AQIM and its allies may have the opportunity to acquire additional territory in the future. They will continue to contest for control of parts of Mali, especially after the French withdraw their troops.
- There is always the potential for AQIM and allied groups to attempt a mass casualty attack in the West. For obvious reasons, most analysts downplay AQIM's capabilities and intent in this regard. Even though its predecessor

organization targeted France as early as 1994, in more recent years the group has not successfully launched a mass casualty attack in the West. However, as we've seen with other al-Qaeda branches, this does not mean that this will continue to be the case in the future. We've seen time and again how various parts of al-Qaeda's global network have ended up attempting attacks on the U.S.[4] AQIM and allied organizations belong to a network that is loyal to al-Qaeda's senior leadership and remains deeply hostile to the West. While most of their assets will be focused over there, in North and West Africa, there is always the potential for some of their resources and fighters to be deployed over here.

- In August, al-Qaeda emir Ayman al-Zawahiri appointed Nasir al-Wuhayshi, the head of Al Qaeda in the Arabian Peninsula (AQAP), to the position of al-Qaeda's general manager. Based on my reading of captured al-Qaeda documents, the general manager's position is responsible for overseeing the operations of al-Qaeda's many branches.[5] Wuhayshi has been in contact with AQIM's top leader, Abdelmalek Droukdel. However, AQIM's emir ignored some of Wuhayshi's advice in the past.[6] That may change now that Wuhayshi is technically Droukdel's superior. This is important because Wuhayshi has proven to be an effective manager capable of running insurgency operations at the same time that his henchmen have plotted attacks against the U.S.

THE AL-QAEDA NETWORK IN NORTH AFRICA

In this section, I briefly outline the structure of al-Qaeda's network in North Africa. The network is comprised of a clandestine apparatus, al-Qaeda's official branch (joined by its allies), as well as the Ansar al Sharia chapters.

Clandestine Network

We must always be mindful that al-Qaeda has maintained a clandestine global network since its inception. Of course, dismantling this network became the prime objective of American intelligence and counterterrorism officials after the September 11, 2001, terrorist attacks. Today, al-Qaeda continues to maintain a covert network. We regularly find traces of it. This network operates in conjunction with groups that are quite open about their allegiance to al-Qaeda.

In August 2012, a report ("Al Qaeda in Libya: A Profile"), prepared by the federal research division of the Library of Congress (LOC) in conjunction with the Defense Department's Combating Terrorism Technical Support Office, outlined the key actors who were secretly pushing al-Qaeda's agenda forward inside Libya.[7]

Al Qaeda's senior leadership (AQSL) in Pakistan has overseen the effort, according to the report's authors. AQSL "issued strategic guidance to followers in Libya and elsewhere to take advantage of the Libyan rebellion." AQSL ordered its followers to "gather weapons," "establish training camps," "build a network in secret," "establish an Islamic state," and institute sharia law in Libya. "AQSL in Pakistan dispatched trusted senior operatives as emissaries and leaders who could supervise building a network," the report notes. They have been successful in establishing "a core network in Libya," but they still act in secret and refrain from using the al-Qaeda name.

The chief "builder" of al-Qaeda's secret endeavor in Libya was an alleged al-Qaeda operative known as Abu Anas al-Libi, according to the report's authors. Al-Libi was captured by U.S. forces in Tripoli in October. Other al-Qaeda actors are identified in the report and they presumably continue to operate in Libya.

It is likely that al-Qaeda maintains covert operations inside the other North African nations as well. In Egypt, a longtime subordinate to Ayman al-Zawahiri named Muhammad Jamal al-Kashef was designated a terrorist by both the U.S. State Department and the United Nations in October.[8] Egyptian authorities found that Jamal was secretly in contact with Zawahiri while also working with al-Qaeda in the Arabian Peninsula (AQAP) and Al Qaeda in the Islamic Maghreb (AQIM). Jamal established training camps in the north Sinai and eastern Libya. And some of his trainees went on to take part in the attack on the U.S. Mission in Benghazi, Libya on September 11, 2012. Jamal is currently jailed inside Egypt, but his upstart branch of al-Qaeda, commonly referred to as the "Muhammad Jamal Network," remains active. Jamal's network has even established ties to terrorists inside Europe.

Jamal's activities prior to his capture highlight the interconnectivity of al-Qaeda's global network, including throughout North Africa and the Middle East, as well as the organization's desire for secrecy in some key respects. In addition to its official and unofficial branches, al-Qaeda has also established and maintained terrorist cells. This has long been part of the organization's tradecraft.

Official Al-Qaeda Branch and Allies

Since the September 11, 2001, terrorist attacks, al-Qaeda's formal branches have grown significantly. Al-Qaeda's official branch, or affiliate, in North Africa is AQIM. While AQIM's predecessor organizations were already closely tied to al-Qaeda, AQIM was officially recognized by Ayman al-Zawahiri in late 2006. AQIM's main objectives have been to overthrow North African governments it said were ruled by apostates and to replace their rule with an Islamic state based on sharia law. The Arab uprisings removed the "infidel" governments, which initially surprised al-Qaeda's ideologues because they did not expect, nor advocate, nonviolent political change. But, in al-Qaeda's view, the task remains unfinished because its harsh brand of sharia law has not been implemented.

Mali was the first instance in which AQIM attempted to govern a large amount of territory based on its sharia code. In taking over two-thirds of Mali, AQIM partnered with other organizations that shared its desire to see sharia implemented. Chief among these is Ansar al-Dine (AAD), which was added to the U.S. Government's list of global terrorist organization in March 2013.[9] The State Department noted that AAD "cooperates closely" with AQIM and "has received support from AQIM since its inception in late 2011." AAD "continues to maintain close ties" to AQIM and "has received backing from AQIM in its fight against Malian and French forces." The U.N.'s official designation page contains additional details concerning the relationship between AAD and AQIM.[10]

Captured AQIM documents further illuminate the relationship between AQIM and AAD. In one "confidential letter" from Abdelmalek Droukdel (the emir of AQIM) to his fighters, Droukdel notes that his forces should be split in two. Part of AQIM's forces would operate under AAD's command in northern Mali while the other part should focus on "external activity," meaning terrorism elsewhere.[11]

Another AQIM-allied group is the Movement for Unity and Jihad in West Africa (MUJAO), which was formed by AQIM commanders who wanted to expand their operations. MUJAO was designated by the U.S. Government as a terrorist organization in December 2012.[12] Still another al-Qaeda-linked group was formed by Mokhtar Belmokhtar, a former senior AQIM who, because of leadership disagreements, formed his own organization in late 2012. In August, Belmokhtar announced that his group, the al-Mulathameen Brigade, had merged with MUJAO.[13]

Despite disagreements between the leaders of these various al-Qaeda-linked groups, they are all openly loyal to al-Qaeda's senior leadership and they have all continued to work closely together in Mali and elsewhere. In addition, Boko Haram, which was also recently designated a terrorist organization, has joined this coalition and is "linked" to AQIM.[14]

Ansar Al Sharia in Egypt, Libya, Tunisia, and Yemen

Two prominent chapters of Ansar al-Sharia have risen in North Africa, one in Libya and the other in neighboring Tunisia. Some have argued that while these Ansar al-Sharia chapters cooperate with al-Qaeda they have fundamentally different goals. Ansar al-Sharia is said to be focused on purely "local" matters, while al-Qaeda is only interested in the global jihad. But this is simply not true. Al-Qaeda's most senior leaders, including Ayman al-Zawahiri, have repeatedly said that one of his organization's chief priorities is to implement sharia law as the foundation for an Islamic state. This is precisely Ansar al-Sharia's goal. In addition, there are credible reports that the Ansar al-Sharia chapters in both Libya and Tunisia have provided recruits for al-Qaeda's affiliates and other jihadist organizations in Syria, the new epicenter for the global jihad.

The very first Ansar al-Sharia chapter was established in Yemen by AQAP. The U.S. Government recognizes Ansar Al Sharia Yemen as simply an "alias" for AQAP.[15] Ansar al-Sharia was part of AQAP's expansion into governance, which involved the implementation of sharia law.

An Ansar al-Sharia chapter in Egypt has hardly concealed its loyalty to al-Qaeda. Its founder, an extremist who has long been tied to al-Qaeda's senior leadership, has said that he is "honored to be an extension of al-Qaeda."[16] Ansar Al Sharia Egypt was formed by members of the Egyptian Islamic Jihad (EIJ), a terrorist organization headed by Ayman al-Zawahiri that also merged with al-Qaeda. Mohammed al-Zawahiri, Ayman's younger brother, starred at Ansar Al Sharia Egypt's events prior to his re-imprisonment. Ansar Al Sharia Egypt's social media has consistently praised and advocated on behalf of al-Qaeda.

In this context, it is hardly surprising to find that the Ansar al-Sharia chapters in Libya and Tunisia behave much like their counterparts. In October, Tunisian Prime Minister Ali Larayedh told Reuters, "There is a relation between leaders of Ansar al-Sharia [Tunisia], Al Qaeda in the Islamic Maghreb and Ansar Al Sharia in Libya. We are coordinating with our neighbors over that."[17] Tunisian officials have repeatedly alleged that Ansar Al Sharia in Tunisia is closely tied to AQIM, and even that they have discovered a handwritten allegiance pact between the emirs of the two organizations. Ansar Al Sharia Tunisia responded to these allegations by confirming its "loyalty" to al-Qaeda while claiming that it remains organizationally independent—a claim that is contradicted by other evidence.[18]

Some of Ansar Al Sharia Tunisia's most senior leaders have known al-Qaeda ties, and at least two of them previously served as important al-Qaeda operatives in Europe.[19] The group's leadership openly praises al-Qaeda. And the organization's social media is littered with pro-al-Qaeda messages. AQIM leaders have repeatedly praised and offered advice to Ansar Al Sharia Tunisia.

Similarly, Ansar Al Sharia Libya's leaders are openly pro-al-Qaeda. The group has denounced the Libyan Government for allowing American forces to capture Abu Anas al-Libi, a top al-Qaeda operative. Ansar al-Sharia has even been running a charity campaign on al-Libi's behalf. The authors of "Al Qaeda in Libya: A Profile," the Library of Congress report published in August 2012, concluded that Ansar Al Sharia Libya "has increasingly embodied al-Qaeda's presence in Libya." And Sufian Ben Qumu, a former Guantanamo detainee who is now an Ansar al-Sharia leader based in Derna, Libya, has longstanding ties to al-Qaeda. A leaked Joint Task Force Guantanamo (JTF–GTMO) threat assessment describes Ben Qumu as an "associate" of Osama bin Laden. JTF–GTMO found that Ben Qumu worked as a driver for a company owned by bin Laden in the Sudan, fought alongside al-Qaeda and the Taliban in Afghanistan, and maintained ties to several other well-known al-Qaeda leaders. Ben Qumu's alias was reportedly found on the laptop of an al-Qaeda operative responsible for overseeing the finances for the September 11, 2001, terrorist attacks. The information on the laptop indicated that Ben Qumu was an al-Qaeda "member receiving family support."[20]

The weight of the evidence makes it far more likely than not that the Ansar al-Sharia chapters in Libya and Tunisia are part of al-Qaeda's network in North Africa. This has important policy ramifications because both groups have been involved in violence, with Ansar Al Sharia Libya taking part in the Benghazi terrorist attack and Ansar Al Sharia Tunisia sacking the U.S. Embassy in Tunis 3 days later. The Tunisian Government has also blamed Ansar al-Sharia for a failed suicide attack, the first inside Tunisia in years. While both chapters have been involved in violence, they have also been working hard to earn new recruits for their organizations and al-Qaeda's ideology. The Arab uprisings created a unique opportunity for them to proselytize.

End Notes

1. "Al-Qaeda in the Islamic Maghreb (AQIM): A Profile," A Report Prepared by the Federal Research Division, Library of Congress under an Interagency Agreement with the Combating Terrorism Technical Support Office's Irregular Warfare Support Program, May 2012. The report's authors described AQIM and jihadists in general as "more a nuisance than an existential threat to the countries in which they operate." However, AQIM certainly became an existential threat to many Muslims in Mali in the months that followed the publication of this report.

2. David Lewis and Laurent Prieur, "Insight: Revival of Islamists in Mali Tests French, U.N. Nerve," Reuters, November 14, 2013; http://www.reuters.com/article/2013/11/14/us-mali-islamists-insight-idUSBRE9AD0QC20131114.

3. See: Agence France Press, "Jihadists Hunted in Tunisia 'Former Mali Fighters'," May 10, 2013; http://www.globalpost.com/dispatch/news/afp/130510/jihadists-hunted-tunisia-former-mali-fighters. Lambroschini, Antoine, "Two Soldiers Killed in Tunisia Hunt for Qaeda-Linked Group," Agence France Presse, June 6, 2013; http://www.google.com/hostednews/afp/article/ALeqM5hlsUffq2sL8NuZjHiPlGA10-WOXA?docId=CNG.89440e74fb0ad05503b0e0f59380c91b.01&hl=en.

4. Prior to the attempted Christmas Day 2009 bombing of Flight 253, Al Qaeda in the Arabian Peninsula (AQAP) was perceived as mainly a threat to Western interests inside Yemen, not abroad. A few months later, in May 2010, a Pakistani Taliban operative attempted to detonate a car bomb in the middle of Times Square. Earlier this year, a plot targeting a commuter train traveling from New York City to Toronto was unraveled by Canadian authorities. The plotters were tied to al-Qaeda's presence inside Iran. The Boston bombings in April show that young men who are drawn to the ideology of al-Qaeda-associated groups in Chechnya and Dagestan can be a threat to the U.S.

5. Thomas Joscelyn and Bill Roggio, "AQAP's Emir Also Serves as Al Qaeda's General Manager," The Long War Journal, August 6, 2013; http://www.longwarjournal.org/archives/2013/08/aqaplemirlalsolserve.php.

6. Bill Roggio, "Wuhayshi Imparted Lessons of AQAP Operations in Yemen to AQIM," The Long War Journal, August 12, 2013; http://www.longwarjournal.org/archives/2013/08/wuhayshilimpartslles.php.

7. A copy of the report can be found online here: http://www.fas.org/irp/world/para/aq-libya-loc.pdf.

8. The State Department's announcement of Jamal's designation can be found here: http://www.state.gov/r/pa/prs/ps/2013/10/215171.htm. The U.N.'s designation page can be viewed here: http://www.un.org/News/Press/docs/2013/sc11154.doc.htm.

43

9. http://www.state.gov/r/pa/prs/ps/2013/03/206493.htm.

10. http://www.un.org/sc/committees/1267/NSQE13513E.shtml.

11. Bill Roggio, ''Al Qaeda in Mali Sought To Hide Foreign Designs,'' The Long War Journal, February 15, 2013; http://www.longwarjournal.org/archives/2013/02/allqaedalinlmalil sou.php.

12. http://www.state.gov/r/pa/prs/ps/2012/12/201660.htm.

13. Bill Roggio, ''Al Qaeda Group Led by Belmokhtar, MUJAO Unite To Form al-Murabitoon,'' Threat Matrix, August 22, 2013; http://www.longwarjournal.org/threat-matrix/archives/2013/08/allqaedalgroupslleadlbylbelmok.php.

14. For details concerning how these various groups, and Boko Haram, have operated alongside one another, see: Jacob Zenn, ''Boko Haram's International Connections,'' CTC Sentinel, January 14, 2013; http://www.ctc.usma.edu/posts/boko-harams-international-connections. See also: Bill Roggio, ''US Adds West African Group, 2 Leaders, to Terrorism List,'' The Long War Journal, December, 7, 2012; http://www.longwarjournal.org/archives/2012/12/usladdslwestl african.php. The designation for Boko Haram, noting it is ''linked'' to AQIM, can be found here: http://www.state.gov/r/pa/prs/ps/2013/11/217509.htm. For more on Boko Haram's ties to the global al-Qaeda network, see: Thomas Joscelyn, ''A Well-Deserved Terrorist Designation,'' The Weekly Standard, November 13, 2013; http://www.weeklystandard.com/blogs/well-deserved-terrorist-designationl767037.html.

15. Thomas Joscelyn, ''State Department: Ansar al-Sharia An Alias for AQAP,'' The Long War Journal, October 4, 2012; http://www.longwarjournal.org/archives/2012/10/stateldepartmentl ans.php.

16. Thomas Joscelyn, ''Ansar al-Sharia Egypt Founder 'Honored To Be An Extension of al-Qaeda,''' The Long War Journal, November 27, 2012; http://www.longwarjournal.org/archives/2012/11/ansarlallsharialegyp.php.

17. Patrick Markey and Tarek Amara, ''Tunisia Sees Islamist Militants Exploiting Libya Chaos,'' Reuters, October 20, 2013; http://articles.chicagotribune.com/2013-10-20/news/sns-rt-us-tunisia-20131020l1lislamist-militants-ansar-al-sharia-libya. It should be noted that one year earlier, during interviews on CNN and Fox News in October 2012, Mike Rogers, the Chairman of the House Intelligence Committee, made similar claims. Rogers said that Ansar al Sharia Tunisia is ''probably'' an al-Qaeda affiliate and that the Ansar al Sharias in Tunisia and Libya are the ''same organization.''

18. Thomas Joscelyn, ''Ansar al-Sharia Responds to Tunisian Government,'' The Long War Journal, September 3, 2013; http://www.longwarjournal.org/archives/2013/09/ansarlall sharialtunil6.php.

19. Thomas Joscelyn, ''Al-Qaeda Ally Orchestrated Assault on U.S. Embassy in Tunisia,'' The Long War Journal, October 2, 2012; http://www.longwarjournal.org/archives/2012/10/allqaedalallylorches.php. See also: Thomas Joscelyn, ''From al-Qaeda in Italy to Ansar al Sharia Tunisia,'' The Long War Journal, November 21, 2012; http://www.longwarjournal.org/archives/2012/11/fromlallqaedalinlita.php.

20. The leaked JTF–GTMO threat assessment can be found on The New York Times Web site: http://projects.nytimes.com/guantanamo/detainees/557-abu-sufian-ibrahim-ahmed-hamuda-bin-qumu/documents/11.

Senator KAINE. Thank you. Boy, that raises a lot of questions.

Let me just start with the regional point, Mr. Joscelyn. You addressed that. We can talk about these nations individually, and I have questions about them individually, but the first panel suggested that there is at least the regional partnership through the Trans-Sahara Counterterrorism Partnership. One of you indicated that that has not really been implemented fully or it has more work to do. And second, the assertion was made by our State Department witness that there is some possibility for using the more functioning civil societies in Algeria and Morocco as sort of models or examples that can help in Tunisia or Libya.

Talk to me about sort of regional prospects before we get into some of the country-specific issues that you raised.

Mr. JOSCELYN. Well, you know, this is where it gets difficult because there are different situations in each country, obviously. I mean, you have a different environment in each country, and I agree with what the panel was saying previously about Tunisia being one of the better hopes for democracy in the region and along those lines.

But I think the fundamental point I have as an al-Qaeda guy, a guy who studies al-Qaeda, is that they do not think about things in terms of state to state. I mean, they do and they do not. They understand that the operating environment in each state is different, but they have regional designs.

And so they are basically going to try and exploit whatever vacuums they can to push forward their agenda. And unless we are having a strong hand—I think Dr. Lawrence is the one who mentioned the light footprint in Libya and Tunisia, which I agree with. I think unless we are having a strong hand in terms of emphasizing that, that this needs to be regional coordination across these countries, I think that that is something that is going to be lost in terms of strategy inside North Africa.

Senator KAINE. Other thoughts on that?

Yes, Dr. Lawrence.

Dr. LAWRENCE. A couple of thoughts. First of all, in terms of tactics and strategies, there was a difference for a while in that for a while Tunisia and Libya got a pass from the worst terrorists in most ways because the successes of the revolutions was seen as giving a space for the possibility of Islamist governments. This has also helped a little bit in Morocco. To the degree to which the terrorists view the country as a potential Islamic state as opposed to a Western-backed secular state, there was a reduction in terrorism as we normally know it.

And it also led to—and I have a paper on it I am happy to submit—the rise of the new jihadi Solifism, which is much less remote terrorists out in the mountains and in the desert and much more a mainstreaming of jihadi Solifist discourse within the cities of people who are living among regular and still espousing that same rhetoric but doing things more like targeted actions against embassies or against intellectuals, writers, that sort of thing, rather than classical terrorism.

So we have seen some pretty major changes because of the Arab Spring. The Algerian Government never got a pass in many ways. Their government was always seen as the fomenter of all this, and that is one of the reasons why a lot of the Arab Spring tumult incubated in Algeria, and I am happy to say more about that.

In terms of regional cooperation, these countries do not want to cooperate with each other much. There are a lot of debates going on about forcing it. We tend to want to see the region as a region, which is why we want it to be an economic region too, because it helps us to have big markets and big regions cooperating. But these guys do not want to cooperate with each other, in part because of big distrust among the countries. I mean, look at Algeria's recent announcement that they are going to be crossing the Tunisian and Libyan border without permission to go after bad guys, which is a violation of their long-standing principle of non-interference either of outsiders in the Algerian state or Algeria and the neighboring states.

So we are seeing Algeria sort of stepping up and playing more of a regional role, but not necessarily in a way that makes us all warm and fuzzy about what is going to be the outcome of Algeria reaching out regionally that way.

In terms of the whole civil society thing, you asked a question about whether the civil societies were better functioning in one country or another, and I would say all the countries have big destabilizing influences, which is why I focused on that in my introductory remarks.

Algeria has over 11,000 deployments of riot police per year. The reason why we did not have a regime change in Algeria gets back to what the previous panel said about the economic strength of the Algerian state, but also because of war weariness, that neither the Algerian security forces nor the population want to push these local grievances into that kind of ferocious combat like they saw in the 1990s.

There are other dynamics in Morocco, and others in Tunisia, and others in Libya, but to think that the quiescence has anything to do with popular satisfaction with the governments, we are not seeing that. The number two vote-getter in the Moroccan election was spoiled ballots. You have similar statistics in Algeria. You have a deep and increasing suspicion of all forces in the Tunisian state. And, of course, in Libya we have this fragmented reality that we are talking about.

In fact, I increasingly think that young people are wondering what types of new institutions they need to build from scratch because there is no faith in existing political parties among the masses of young people, and little faith in civil society, which has long been controlled by governments in this part of the world.

Senator KAINE. Thank you.

Dr. Wehrey, do you want to say a word about the regional efforts? Then I want to come back and ask you a question about militias.

Dr. WEHREY. Absolutely. Well, with regard to Libya's cooperation, it is very problematic given the informal security sector. I mean, the militias are controlling so much of the country on the borders, and this impacts, for instance, Algeria's willingness to cooperate on border security. The Algerians are convinced that the Libyan Government is penetrated by Islamists, whom they fear, and they are really loathe to cooperate.

Regarding Libyan and Egyptian relations, there is intense distrust in Libya regarding Egypt's supposed sponsorship of Gadhafi loyalists in the country. With the CC government now, there are sensitivities among many Libyan Islamists about that government. Libya has had, I think, better cooperation with some of the countries to the south—for instance, Chad.

But again, when we are talking about regional cooperation, we are talking about interactions between states, state institutions, and Libya just does not have those institutions in place.

Senator KAINE. Let us go to the militia testimony that you gave earlier. First, just help me understand. When we hear 300 militias, it is a little hard for us to get our head around. I have not traveled to Libya as you have spent so much time doing. Are these militias primarily sort of geographical and town- and community-based? Are they ethnic-based? How would you describe kind of their formation?

Dr. WEHREY. The majority of them are based on town or region. They range anywhere from 200 to really no more than perhaps 2,000 men. Many of them arose during the revolution. They were the fighting units that overthrew Gadhafi. But others arose after the revolution, and in some cases they are more opportunistic gangs. I mean, they have gotten into criminal enterprise.

So there are ones that have allied themselves for political reasons with politicians in the Parliament. There are those that are effectively sort of Neighborhood Watch programs for towns where there is no municipal police, there is no government forces providing security.

In the east, for instance, the militias are demanding federalism. They are demanding a greater share of the oil revenues. They have shut down oil production. So as we have heard, in each of Libya's regions, the militias fulfill a different role.

In the far south among some of these ethnic communities, the Tebu and the Taureg, the militias do have an ethnic component there.

Senator KAINE. And do you agree with Dr. Lawrence's earlier testimony that it is not right to look at Libyan instability as sort of a single kind of instability but, depending on where it is in the country, there are all kinds of reasons for instabilities that you might see?

Dr. WEHREY. Absolutely. I mean, there are many different microconflicts going on in Libya right now that reflect the legacy of Gadhafi's rule. He pitted communities against one another. He played them off, and we are seeing these manifest themselves.

For instance, in the east, in Benghazi, what is happening there, these assassinations is a shadowy mix of Islamists and criminals, vendettas against the old regime. The militia problem there is really qualitatively different than what is happening in Tripoli, where you have two power centers, Zintan and Misrata, that are essentially laying siege to the capital, demanding the spoils of the revolution. I mean, they are claiming ministries, they are kicking out the army, and we have seen over the weekend some of these militias pull back. But whether that really represents a dismantling of the militias I think remains to be seen.

Senator KAINE. And just using the Tripoli example that each of you talked about in your testimony, it was an anti militia protest. Forty-six individuals who were protesting were killed. But then I gather even after that there was additional civilian protest to really continue to amplify the message that we want the militias out. And has that continued?

Dr. WEHREY. Absolutely. There were civil strikes. I mean, the city was shut down, shops were closed, there were more protests, and what you did see was the deployment of the army into Tripoli. People were wondering, where has the army been all this time? So you did see the government finally deploy the army. You had some negotiations where militias have pulled out of the capital, outside the capital. But does this really represent diminishment of militia strength I think remains to be seen.

The army—I mean, this was a show of force, but can the army really sustain itself? The army does not match the militias in terms of manpower or firepower.

Senator KAINE. You had a five-point kind of plan that you walked through, and I think the final point was to try to basically deemphasize the militias and to get them out of the militias and to reintegrate militia members back into civilian life.

Dr. WEHREY. Right.

Senator KAINE. And I gather that you put that fifth because it might be the hardest thing to do, and you could probably only do it if you did the other four steps first. Do I read that right?

Dr. WEHREY. It is the most difficult. I mean, this is an entrenched economic and social problem. The Libyan Government has developed a program to try to identify young men in the militias and to register them, to get them into jobs and scholarships. But this program has fallen victim to political in-fighting, to lack of funding, but it is a good first step. As I understand it, multiple U.S. agencies are supporting this effort to really get at the roots of this problem and to show these young men that you fought in the revolution, but now is the time to move on and build the country and relinquish your arms.

Senator KAINE. I am going to ask a similar question, Mr. Joscelyn, to you, and then Dr. Lawrence, but kind of each in your own sphere. So with respect to your focus on al-Qaeda, based on your experience, would it be your recommendation that our policy should be to do new things or to do more of the things that we are currently doing? Do we need to look at a different strategy other than the current Trans-Sahara Counterterrorism Partnership, or do we just need to make heavier investments in the activities that we are currently doing in order to counter the extremist influence?

Mr. JOSCELYN. Well, I think my big warning is that I find these groups do have plans for what they are doing, and my beginning point is to figure out what that plan is, and then our plan is to basically dismantle it. That is essentially where we start.

So when we talk about militias, for example, there is good evidence that this was part of al-Qaeda's plan for inside Libya, to coopt or work with certain militias. These militias are not going to reintegrate into a more national force. Identifying and isolating and trying to contain those militias should be part of any strategy for anything we are doing inside Libya. In fact, I warned in April 2011 about some of these militias in congressional testimony as having already been coopted by al-Qaeda, and some of them went on to take part, including Ansar al-Sharia, in the Benghazi terrorist attack.

So to that extent and just to play off something that Dr. Lawrence said a few minutes ago, too, he was exactly right. When I said that they do and they do not view it regionally, they have a whole comprehensive strategy for the region, our enemies do, but how they operate in any given country can vary, absolutely. So that is part of how we have to adjust our tactics, that it corresponds to what they are doing.

For example, in Tunisia, for a long time they would like to talk about Ansar al-Sharia was basically doing charity events. I was very concerned about this because these are not overt acts of terrorism, of course, but yet what they are doing is they are building up their cadre which can be used for those types of terrorist acts in the future. Now what we have seen is that, in fact, they had a clandestine apparatus that was planning and plotting terrorism all along, including, in fact, the ransacking of our Embassy.

Senator KAINE. And, Dr. Lawrence, your focus is really on— I mean, a focus on young people and what we need to do. So I gather your answer to my question is not that we need to do more of what we are doing but we kind of need to do different things and have a different focus that really is looking at the youth in the region.

Dr. LAWRENCE. Yes, and the youth are everybody. I mean, basically because of the youth bulge, we are talking about the entirety of these populations. The median age in Tunisia, which has turned the demographic corner, is 30. In Morocco and Algeria it is 27, and in Libya it is 24. So the latter three suffer more from that structural youth bulge problem. In Tunisia, it is more about unemployed university graduates that is the destabilizing factor demographically.

Four very quick points.

During the revolution in Libya, almost every community liberated itself, and that is why the militias are community-based, except Tripoli, which 80 percent liberated itself in 24 hours in August 2011, and then the Zintanis and the Misratans finished off the job in 9 days with the help of NATO and never left.

So one of the things that is unique about Tripoli is that you had foreign militias that never left. So kicking the Misratans out of Tripoli is progress, but it does not solve any other problem, except that civilians across Libya, insofar as they have other problem militias, will see this as an example. But this was the only problem with militias from somewhere else.

A second point is that there was some work done by Small Arms Survey, in cooperation with Crisis Group, and we did a taxonomy of the militias, and I agree with everything that Fred said. But just to give you a little data point, about 80 percent of the militias were the revolutionary militias that now work for the government, and they are getting in trouble with the government all the time because they are not getting paid or because there is some political policy they do not like, so they will storm Parliament or they will hold a minister hostage. But these are the pro-revolutionary militias. In our coverage we conflate the pro-revolutionary militias that are causing a lot of the ruckus with everybody else. It is different militias.

About 10 percent of the militias are these post-revolutionary militias that tended to be from the more pro-Gadhafi areas, like Bani Walid, and they have another set of issues. And then about 5 percent of the militias are unaffiliated either way, and they are basically kids with arms doing something. And then the other 5 percent are terroristic and criminal gangs, some of which predated the revolution and which continue to cause all the types of problems that Mr. Joscelyn is talking about. But you have to think about these four different types of militias.

The third point is the GPF is a great idea and I subscribe to everything that Fred said, but the metaphor I use for Libya, both before and after the revolution because I have worked on Libya since the early 2000s, is that you do not want to put all your eggs in the GPF basket. The metaphor is a train station. It is like we have a GPF train that has not left yet, and then we think all the passengers should get on the GPF train, and we do not know if that track is blocked or whether it will make it.

With Libya, since there is so much dysfunctionality and lack of capacity in government, you have to have several different plans, and you do not know which one is going to move forward at a particular time.

And the last point is to underscore stuff that Fred said. The militias are not going to give up their weapons in Libya, even the very pro-government ones, until we have a situation that is working, we have a constitution, we have further elections, and we have a system that seems less corrupt in which the money starts to flow, and that gets to sort of an economic point, which is that right now oil production is down to 10 percent of peak capacity because of the problems with the militias who were not getting paid.

There are certain enlightened people, like the head of the Tripoli Brigades, who was trying to spin off fighters with microloans to start businesses and that sort of thing. But there is almost no capacity in the government to create economic opportunities for militiamen, and right now one of the best paid jobs for young persons is to be in a militia, getting paid eventually by the government, when they pay you.

So a lot of overlapping problems here, and just kicking the militias out from somewhere is not going to solve them.

Senator KAINE. Let me just follow up on that. I do not think it was stated so unequivocally in the first panel, but to some degree they did. There is sort of an assumption that Libya does not need financial assistance because it has natural resources. Is that your view as well, or does the diminished oil production and other sort of economic challenges and militiamen not getting paid—I mean, is there a need for us with our partners to contemplate financial assistance?

Dr. LAWRENCE. On this score, it is the same in Libya before the revolution—and I worked in a lot of cooperative programs with Libya—as Libya after the revolution, poor governmental capacity and a big mistrust of foreigners coming in with a plan for Libya. So the way in which you do successful cooperation with Libya is you pilot stuff.

Senator KAINE. Pilot.

Dr. LAWRENCE. And to pilot things, you have to have resources. I was often flummoxed when I worked at the State Department and I talked to Congress and others back when I worked for the government that they would say OK—and you hear this in national organizations, too—Libya has money, so we do not need money. The problem is that in order to get Libya to take out its checkbook and pay for things—and right now the bank balance is very low because of the crisis in oil sales—you need to demonstrate to the Libyans what works and who the good people are to work with. And to do that, the United Nations, the European Union, the United States, and other friends and partners with Libya have to spend a little bit of money to pilot things. And if things are successful on the pilot level, then the Libyans will take out their checkbook and start paying for things.

The same with Algeria, which has $120 billion in the bank and is not spending it. So you have a very rich country with very low spending in the areas that it needs to be spending, and it needs international cooperation to help point the way.

Morocco and Tunisia is a different dynamic.

Senator KAINE. Let me just ask one last question both for Dr. Joscelyn and Dr. Wehrey, or Mr. Joscelyn and Dr. Wehrey.

Dr. Lawrence in his testimony talked a little bit about the Syria effect, folks coming back, some backlash from Syria. Mr. Joscelyn, you just alluded to it briefly in your testimony. But I would like you to each talk about how you see instability in Syria or other regional instabilities kind of washing back into the Maghreb.

Mr. JOSCELYN. Well, one of the things that happened with Al Qaeda in the Islamic Maghreb is that its operations accelerated during the Iraq war because they were sending off a lot of recruits to fight in Iraq. Currently during the Syrian war, basically we have seen that same pattern. Many of those same facilitation networks are being used to send recruits from North Africa to Syria to fight, and they can obviously bring them back to North Africa or they can raise trouble and create problems in their home countries.

One of the things that I have seen evidence of is, for example, the Ansar al-Sharia branches in Tunisia and Libya appear to be sending off recruits to Syria. They actually promote this sort of thing. I see it in their social media. I see it in various different indications.

So these are groups that are very actively sending off recruits to fight in Syria and elsewhere. The reason why that is important is because it shows you that, again, to the whole idea that there is a network. There is a network in play of individuals across this region, and even into the Middle East, that is capable of sort of orchestrating terrorism, and it is not just about the insurgency in Syria that these guys are fighting, but it can also be used in other ways to manifest itself. It is having effects in Iraq. It could potentially have effects in Turkey or throughout the region, the Middle East and elsewhere.

Senator KAINE. Dr. Wehrey.

Dr. WEHREY. Well, I certainly agree. I mean, there is activity by some of these radical Islamist groups, Ansar al-Sharia, the Omar Mukhtar Brigade in the east, that send volunteers. These individuals are participating with al-Qaeda-affiliated units in Syria. But there is also, I think, a broader movement in Libya of sending volunteers out of Islamist nationalism that is not really al-Qaeda. They are fighting with the Free Syrian Army. I mean, these people did go to Afghanistan and Iraq, and they see an impulse to help suffering Muslims in Syria, but they are not al-Qaeda, and I do not think there is going to be a threat from them coming back.

I do think it is important to distinguish in Libya right now, when you look at the Islamist spectrum, that the al-Qaeda affiliates or sympathizers is a very small minority. Many of these Islamists, they did fight in Afghanistan, they did fight against United States Forces in Iraq, but they have come back and they have integrated into the political system. I mean, they have offices. They are in the Cabinet. They are in Parliament. I think it is a good thing.

You hear this narrative in Libya by many politicians to try to tar all Islamists as either Brotherhood or al-Qaeda, and I think that is very, very dangerous, and we need to distinguish it.

Senator KAINE. Well, I want to thank you all for your testimony. It was great to hear the first panel, which was all State Department, DOD, AID, talking about what we are doing. Your value is having an expertise and an independence to kind of not just talk about what we are doing but assess what is working and what is not. It was helpful to have you today, and I appreciate it.

And with that, the hearing is adjourned.

[Whereupon, at 3:59 p.m., the hearing was adjourned.]

ADDITIONAL MATERIAL SUBMITTED FOR THE RECORD

RESPONSES OF PRINCIPAL DEPUTY ASSISTANT SECRETARY RICHARD SCHMIERER TO QUESTIONS SUBMITTED BY SENATOR ROBERT MENENDEZ

MIDDLE EAST AND NORTH AFRICA TRANSITION FUND

Question. If funding was appropriated for the Transition Fund, what programs, activities, and types of engagement would be funded?

Answer. During the 2012 U.S. Presidency of the G8 Deauville Partnership with Arab Countries in Transition, the United States led an effort to design and launch a new, grant-based Middle East and North Africa Transition Fund to support technical assistance and pilot projects in the areas of economic governance; trade, investment, and integration; and inclusive development and job creation.

The Fund's mandate is to provide funding for projects that will allow transition governments participating in the Deauville Partnership (Tunisia, Libya, Jordan, Morocco, Yemen, and Egypt) to make tangible progress on policy reforms critical to promoting economic stability and enabling a shift toward democracy. Projects can support ministries, local municipalities, central banks, and Parliaments, and many of the projects proposed are aimed at improving governments' capacity to support small and medium enterprises, youth employment, and engage with civil society. Transition countries and multilateral development banks jointly produce proposals that the Fund's steering committee selects through a competitive process to create incentives for innovation and solid program design.

To date, the Fund has approved $101 million for 24 projects in the partnership countries, and an additional $36 million will be available for additional project approvals by the end of the year. Other donors (not including the United States) have pledged $156 million, of which they have disbursed $117 million to date. By the end of this calendar year, the United States will have provided $20 million to the MENA Transition Fund, of which $10 million was provided in May 2013. Examples of actions to be taken by recipient governments in North Africa as a result of projects financed by the Fund include:

• Tunisia: Establish an Investment Authority to increase investments in the country, creating much needed jobs and boosting economic growth.
  • Morocco: Develop a new governance framework based on public consultation, transparent budgets, and fiscal decentralization.

SMART POWER

Question. How has the State Department changed the way it does business since 2011 in order to engage with North African Youth, including the next generation, including Fulbright and other scholarship opportunities?

Answer. Prior to and after the Arab Spring, the State Department's Public Diplomacy programming in North Africa has sought to expand constructive political, commercial, security, and people-to-people partnerships, and to apply the themes of pluralism, transparency, and fairness in ways that recognize the diversity of local circumstances and audiences across the region. Given increasing levels of unemployment in the post-Arab Awakening period, especially among those under the age of 30, U.S. Public Diplomacy programming also encourages North African youth to seek expanded opportunities through education, entrepreneurship, and professional development.

We have also used public-private partnerships to promote entrepreneurship, education, investment, youth employment and regional economic cooperation throughout the Maghreb. Since 2010, our partnerships provided an effective framework for regular exchanges of experience and expertise among U.S. Government representatives, prominent American business leaders and local entrepreneurs.

Over the past 2 years in Libya, Embassy Tripoli has supported English Access Microscholarship Programs in Tripoli and Benghazi, and EducationUSA advisors at six universities. Ambassador Jones signed a memorandum of understanding on higher education cooperation with the Libyan Government in the fall of 2013. Social media also greatly enhances the mission's reach; its 220,000 Facebook fans make Embassy Tripoli one of the top-five subscribed pages in the country.

Positive trends in the PD environment have continued to support a level U.S. engagement with the Tunisian people and government that would have been unimaginable under the previous regime. A key program in Tunis is the U.S.-funded Thomas Jefferson Scholars program, which will send about 300 students to the United States over 3 years for a year of undergraduate or community college study. When combined with the over 20 active partnership programs between U.S. and Tunisian universities, Embassy Tunis is making considerable and rapid inroads in Tunisian higher education. The English Access Microscholarship Program is now active in eight cities, reaching 1,000 underprivileged teenagers.

The stable environment and enthusiastic support of the Moroccan Government have made Morocco an ideal testing ground for new PD programs, including the English Access Microscholarship and the Youth Exchange and Study Programs, over the past decade. The TechCamp Caravan Program, which has already provided intensive technology training to over 120 Moroccan NGOs, is emblematic of an outreach strategy that seeks to educate, entertain, engage, and empower audiences in every corner of Morocco. Another public diplomacy program highlighted the economic and health impacts of counterfeit pharmaceutical and consumer products to youths just beginning to form their market preferences. The program received extensive media coverage over a 2-week period, culminating in a documentary that aired on Morocco's largest television network.

Building on a strong commercial relationship and burgeoning security partnership, Embassy Algiers' Public Diplomacy programming aims to demonstrate the benefits of a closer relationship to citizens and government officials throughout Africa's largest country. Diligent negotiation with the Algerian Government has led to a blossoming partnership in the media, education, arts, and youth programs. In addition to a large English Access Microscholarship Program, Embassy Algiers grants also now provide English training at several government-run youth centers and career skills training at public universities.

Question. What bilateral and regional tools and pressure is the administration using to combat the destabilizing effects of extremist groups such as Al Qaeda in the Islamic Maghreb (AQIM)?

Answer. Combating violent extremist groups, such as AQIM, is a priority for the Obama administration. The Trans-Sahara Counterterrorism Partnership (TSCTP) is the U.S. Government's multiyear, interagency, and regional program designed to build the capacity and resilience of the governments and communities in the Sahel and Maghreb regions of Africa to contain, degrade, and ultimately defeat the threat posed by al-Qaeda, its affiliates, and other violent extremist organizations (VEOs) in the Trans-Sahara region. TSCTP also provides a platform to improve regional and international cooperation and information-sharing, including between the Sahel and Maghreb regions, to counter shared threats. TSCTP partner countries include Algeria, Burkina Faso, Chad, Mali, Mauritania, Morocco, Niger, Nigeria, Senegal, and Tunisia.

The TSCTP budget request for FY 2014 is $45 million. These funds will enable us to build capacity and assist regional counterterrorism (CT) efforts across a large and diverse geographical area with complex security situations. Areas of support include: (1) enabling and enhancing the capacity of North and West African militaries to conduct counterterrorism operations; (2) integrating the ability of North and West African militaries, and other supporting allies, to operate regionally and collaboratively on CT efforts; (3) enhancing individual nations' border security capacity to monitor, restrain, and interdict terrorist movements; (4) strengthening the rule of law, including access to justice, and law enforcement's ability to detect, disrupt, respond to, investigate, and prosecute terrorist activity; (5) monitoring and countering the financing of terrorism (such as that related to kidnapping for ransom); and (6) reducing the limited sympathy and support among communities for violent extremism. Additionally the United States supports countries in the region through bilateral International Military Education and Training (IMET) Programs, which seek to help professionalize their respective militaries, and training and equipment funded from Foreign Military Financing (FMF), which often supports or sustains the capacity of foreign militaries toward achieving counterterrorism goals.

Other programs aimed to combat AQIM and other VEOs include the Department of State's Antiterrorism Assistance (ATA) Program, which provides capacity-building programs for law enforcement agencies of partner nations. All these training programs are designed to institutionalize and sustain improved antiterrorism prevention and response. In the Maghreb region, our ATA training and equipment programs aim to build partner nations' law enforcement capacity, particularly in the areas of border security and investigations.

With the growing youth population and burgeoning unemployment in the region, the United States also supports initiatives that deter youth from participating in terrorist networks, through programs designed to counter violent extremism (CVE). These programs provide positive alternatives to communities most at risk of recruitment and radicalization to violence, through activities like educational opportunities and job trainings, or others that address specific drivers of radicalization; and counter terrorist narratives and the violent extremist worldview by promoting non-violent interpretations of Islam.

Question. What soft power methods is the State Department using to compete with and defeat the ideology and recruitment opportunities exploited by AQIM and other extremist groups?

Answer. Public Diplomacy (PD) Programs are used in the NEA region to counter violent extremism (CVE) by promoting alternatives to violence, providing economic and educational opportunities for marginalized populations, and countering the specific narratives of extremist organizations with positive messages. Throughout North Africa—especially in transition countries—programs are aimed at encouraging broad participation in national political and transition processes, particularly among youth and women. Training, skills development, and education programs enhance economic opportunities for at-risk youth and expand our access to target communities such as religious scholars. In addition, programs are designed to build the capacity of emerging local NGOs. Finally, CVE messaging is accomplished through film and broadcasting initiatives and an active array of social media outreach and messaging tools. Online, the interagency Center for Strategic Counterterrorism Communications' (CSCC) Digital Outreach Team actively engages audiences in North Africa to counter AQIM propaganda. CSCC has produced videos to counter-AQIM and they have been seen by over 57,000 viewers on YouTube alone. Programs aimed at journalism professionalization and civil society organization (CSO) capacity development aid in our long-term ability to partner with local media and CSOs to accomplish CVE goals. English-language training programs are a critical and widely deployed tool in this area and are gaining in popularity and effectiveness.

TUNISIA

Question. The national dialogue, in which all parties have committed to participate in drafting a new constitution and electoral law and selecting an interim government to prepare new elections, has stalled over disagreements concerning the choice of interim Prime Minister. All parties remain committed to the dialogue, but the 4–6 week timetable for the dialogue is very ambitious.

♦ What is the 2013–14 plan for the Tunisian American Enterprise Fund, and what sectors will it focus on?

Answer. The Tunisian-American Enterprise Fund (TAEF) was incorporated on February 4, 2013, and is currently capitalized at $40 million in U.S. foreign assistance funding. The investment has enabled the TAEF to take the necessary first steps to establish an office in Washington, DC, and hire a Tunisian Chief Operations Officer who will set up an office in Tunisia, possibly by the end of 2013. The existing board members held two board meetings in October 2013 to discuss their investment strategy and are expected to finalize and share it with us soon. The TAEF expects to make its first investment in 2014.

The fund will accomplish its objectives by creating and coinvesting in a small number of special purpose mechanisms and joint ventures, alongside for-profit companies and multilateral development banks. TAEF's initial investment focus will be in SME, finance, technology, agriculture, health, and education sectors. These areas would allow the TAEF to target U.S. and international partners' interventions in the Tunisian economy and leverage them for greater economic impact.

Based on prior experience, enterprise funds can take up to 2 years before making investments. The time allows enterprise funds to build a greater understanding of the country's investment environment, explore investment opportunities, and perform due diligence before investing.

Question. What types of U.S. assistance, security and otherwise, have been most effective since 2011 in addressing Tunisia's security challenges and promoting economic and political reform, and an active civil society?

Answer. United States assistance to Tunisia is intended to support Tunisia's democratic transition. Security assistance is a primary focus of our ongoing assistance programs, particularly in countering regional terrorist groups and in reorienting the Ministry of Interior, an institution that was largely associated with the former dictatorial regime. Security assistance programs have bolstered the Tunisian military's ability to obtain and maintain equipment necessary to secure its borders and locate terrorist suspects. Our Foreign Military Financing and International Military Education and Training programs also focus on providing leadership and counterterrorism training to Ministry of Defense officials.

State Department programs, in partnership with the Tunisian Ministries of Interior and Justice, have been effective in supporting leadership development, police reform, antiterrorism training and nonlethal crowd control techniques in Tunisia.

Supporting Tunisia's economic reform is also a priority for the United States. USAID programs work to address some of the constraints and support economic growth. Effective assistance programs that focus on economic reform include the Information and Communications Technology (ICT) Competitiveness Project, which generated over 2,400 jobs for Tunisians and assisted Tunisia in reforming its Tax Code. Other economic programs have focused on developing Tunisia's small and medium-sized enterprises and creating the market space for this sector to flourish, including facilitating loans to small enterprises.

Governance and democracy programming remains an assistance priority. The State Department and USAID contributed significant technical support to the 2011 Tunisian elections and are preparing to provide support for Tunisia's upcoming election as well.

Our assistance also provides Tunisian political parties with training to build relationships with constituents and better articulate the aspirations of the Tunisian people. These programs have been highly effective in ensuring that Tunisian youth are taking on political and civic leadership roles in the ongoing democratic transition as well as in assisting nascent political parties to develop party platforms and constituent communication skills.

Question. What is the administration doing to provide business and investment incentives to support a democratic transition in Tunisia?

Answer. Assistance to help Tunisia expand economic growth and opportunity to all citizens, including through helping Tunisia to develop a better investment climate, is a key component of our ongoing support for Tunisia's democratic transition.

The United States provided $100 million to directly pay debt that Tunisia owed the International Financial Institutions (IFES) allowing the Tunisian Government to accelerate economic growth and job creation. The United States also provided a $30 million loan guarantee that supported $485 million in new, more affordable, financing for the Tunisian Government, strengthening Tunisia's capacity to manage its transition to an economically sound and prosperous democracy.

The United States is focused on providing additional support to Small and Medium Enterprises (SMEs). We have provided $40 million to the Tunisian-American Enterprise Fund, a private, nonprofit corporation to promote the development of the Tunisian private sector with a particular focus on SMEs. The Overseas Private Investment Corporation is also developing a facility of $50 million to provide working capital to Tunisian franchises, many of which will be small businesses. In addition to financial support, we are administering a program to provide technical assistance directly to SMEs. The focus is on supporting SMEs as exporters and providing diagnostic assessments and business facilitation services.

We also engage in activities that support entrepreneurship and innovation within the Tunisian economy. For example, our information and communications technology (ICT) Competitiveness Project provides technical assistance, training, and access to finance for firms in ICT and ICT-enabled sectors (textiles, specialty foods, automotive and other manufacturing) that have the potential to create jobs. Additionally, we are supporting projects that assist the Tunisian Government to boost growth and youth employment in vulnerable, interior regions by promoting youth-led enterprise creation and development, including an emphasis on agricultural, ICT, and environmental sectors.

In order to create a more conducive environment for investment and business, we are engaged in building the capacity of institutions and in working to spur needed economic reforms. The United States is providing technical assistance to improve legislative and regulatory frameworks and the overall business environment, as well as supporting the legal, trade, and investment capacity-building. Additional programs are providing training to build the capacity of 24 existing small business centers located throughout the country, including the interior, in order to improve growth in the SME sector.

Question. Please provide an update on the activities of the Office of Transition Initiatives (USAID), the Middle East Partnership Initiative (State) and other political transition assistance we are carrying out in Tunisia.

Answer. In support of Tunisia's democratic transition, prosperity, and long-term political stability, U.S. assistance continues to strengthen civil society and civic participation in the political process, support a free and fair electoral process, and promote an inclusive transitional justice process.

USAID's Office of Transition Initiatives (OTI) continues programs throughout Tunisia. Specific efforts by OTI have focused on encouraging broad participation in the political transition with a particular emphasis on youth and women's engagement and working with local organizations to identify and respond to community priorities.

To date, OTI has 214 activities completed or currently under implementation. Illustrative examples of OTI activities include: conducting a nationwide tolerance campaign through TV, billboards, and social media; stimulating dialogue between the Constituent Assembly and youth civil society leaders through a forum focused on the role of decentralization and the development of local democracy; facilitating townhall meetings between government officials and communities; encouraging greater activism among women in the interior region during Women's Day; providing physical and virtual meeting space for civil society to conduct business; conducting a live television debate on emerging political issues; and developing art and music workshops for at-risk youth.

The Middle East Partnership Initiative (MEPI) is providing assistance that strengthens political parties and supports elections. Such assistance includes candidate training, voter and civic education designed to increase political participation of marginalized groups, direct assistance to the Tunisian elections management board, and elections observation support.

For example, at the request of the Tunisian Ministry of Youth, MEPI programming has trained 48 government officials from all 24 governorates in order to increase the Ministry's capacity to effectively engage marginalized youth in the political process. MEPI assistance is closely coordinated with USAID and other donors, such as MEPI's joint effort with the United Nations Development Program to help Tunisians develop an electoral law for the next national elections scheduled to be held in 2014.

MOROCCO

Question. Our relationship with Morocco is strong, and it is the only country on the African Continent with which we have a Free Trade Agreement. The unresolved Western Sahara dispute is a barrier to further economic and security cooperation in the region.

♦   How does the administration plan to develop and deepen the 2012 Strategic Dialogue with Morocco?

Answer. The Strategic Dialogue was launched in 2012 out of a shared desire to find opportunities to strengthen the partnership between Morocco and the United States and to seek new avenues for cooperation in the political, security, economic, educational, and cultural spheres. The administration plans to hold a second Strategic Dialogue meeting in early 2014 to build on continuing engagement, to review ongoing activities and identify new joint initiatives in support of the reform efforts being undertaken by His Majesty King Mohammed VI, and to advance our shared priorities of a secure, stable, and prosperous North Africa and Middle East.

Question. Please provide a brief update on Moroccan civil society reforms, particularly those contained in the 2011 constitutional reform.

Answer. Under King Mohammed VI, the Moroccan Government has undertaken a number of economic, social, and political reforms, including a revised constitution that is generally considered a step toward enhanced political rights and transparent governance in Morocco. Since the ratification of the 2011 constitution, the Moroccan Government has made measured progress in the development of the organic laws that the constitution outlines as the foundation for basic rights and the function of the government itself. Thus far, 4 of the 19 articles of the constitution requiring organic laws have been fully addressed by the Parliament. In his October 11, 2013, address to open Parliament's fall session, the King urged the Parliament to pass more of these organic laws.

The 2011 constitution also gives the judiciary greater independence. In September 2013 the High Commission for Judicial Reform and the Ministry of Justice presented their recommendations for judicial reform to King Mohammed VI. The recommendations included an overview of all planned reforms, while highlighting and prioritizing those laws that can be submitted to Parliament before the end of 2013. These changes include greater independence of the judiciary and creation of an accompanying High Judicial Council; a statute that regulates the profession of magistracy; the creation of a Constitutional Court; and changes to the jurisdiction of military tribunals.

Morocco has also taken important steps to promote gender equality. The 2011 constitution called for civic, social, and political equality for women. The laws implementing these changes are working their way through Parliament.

With regard to civil society in particular, civil society organizations are constitutionally empowered to affect political change in Morocco, and key parts of the government are keen to engage citizens in policymaking. Morocco's legal framework for civil society is among the most progressive in the region and given this opportunity, we would like to see the development of clear mechanisms to enable the Moroccan Government to receive input from civil society and facilitate inclusion of civil society in governance processes.

Question. Please describe U.S. policy on the Western Sahara and updates on U.S. support to the U.N. Process.

Answer. The U.S. Government continues to support the process led by U.N. Secretary General Ban Ki-moon and his Personal Envoy for Western Sahara, Christopher Ross, to find a peaceful, sustainable, and mutually agreed solution to the Western Sahara conflict. The U.S. Government, along with all the other members of the Security Council, unanimously adopted Resolution 2099 this year, which took note of the Moroccan autonomy proposal presented to the Secretary General on April 11, 2007, and welcomed the credible Moroccan efforts to move the process forward toward a resolution. It also took note of the Frente Polisario proposal presented on April 10, 2007. The United States has made clear that Morocco's autonomy plan is serious, realistic, and credible, and that it represents a potential approach that could satisfy the aspirations of the people in the Western Sahara to run their own affairs in peace and dignity.

In November 2012 and March and October of this year, the U.N. Secretary General's Personal Envoy held broad-based consultations with the parties to the conflict, Morocco and the Frente Polisario, as well as with important regional stakeholders Algeria and Mauritania. He also consulted with the Friends of Western Sahara (France, Spain, Russia, the United Kingdom, and the United States). Ambassador Ross' work to bring the two parties together continues to hold promise and inspires hope for progress toward the resolution of this conflict. The United States supports Ambassador Ross' approach of bilateral talks with the parties with the aim to launch shuttle diplomacy to work toward finding a just, lasting, and mutually acceptable political solution.

Question. How might the U.S. support a more active Moroccan role in addressing regional security threats? Please describe the state of security cooperation with Morocco date and plans to strengthen this partnership.

Answer. Security cooperation with Morocco is excellent. The United States and Morocco have numerous shared regional priorities throughout the Middle East, North Africa, and the Sahel.

Morocco and the United States have worked together over the past 2 years on the U.N. Security Council for the advancement of international peace and security, including in Mali, the Sahel, Syria, Libya, and the greater Middle East. During their meeting on November 22, 2013, President Obama and King Mohammed VI committed to continuing close cooperation in the Global Counterterrorism Forum and to work to strengthen regional political, economic, and security ties across North Africa and the Sahel, including through a reinvigorated Arab Maghreb Union and other regional forums.

Plans to strengthen this partnership include encouraging Morocco to join the United States in founding the International Institute of Justice and the Rule of Law in Malta, which the President did during his meeting with His Majesty the King. This institute will train a new generation of criminal justice officials across North, West, and East Africa on how to address counterterrorism and related security challenges through a rule of law framework.

ALGERIA

Question. The administration has encouraged Algeria to take a greater role in regional security efforts in the Sahel, including in Mali since 2012. Algeria's political culture remains dominated by the same ruling National Liberation Front generation of leaders who took over at independence in 1962. President Abdelaziz Bouteflika's health has deteriorated dramatically in 2013, and Presidential elections are due to take place in spring 2014, possibly pushing for a fourth term for Bouteflika.

♦ What steps has the administration taken to encourage greater political and economic openness in Algeria?

Answer. The U.S.-Algeria civilian relationship has rapidly expanded and continues to grow today. The United States works closely with our Algerian partners to improve fiscal transparency, and the United States and Algeria actively discuss Algeria's WTO accession bid and our bilateral Trade and Investment Framework Agreement through the U.S.-Algeria Strategic Dialogue. The United States also supports Algerian civil society through a variety of Middle East Partnership Initiative Programs, including a training program for newly elected women parliamentarians and a capacity-building initiative of domestic Civil Society organizations to observe future elections. Additional projects focus on Algerian-led advocacy for critical economic reforms and political leadership capacity building for youth party leaders.

Question. How can we best support Algeria as it takes a larger regional lead in security and counterterrorism efforts?

Answer. The United States and Algeria are already implementing agreements regarding information-sharing, increased training and capacity-building, and political and economic cooperation. Specifically, the United States is working to increase capacity-building programs with Algeria through the Bureau of International Narcotics and Law Enforcement, Anti-Terrorism Assistance Programs, and the Trans-Saharan Counterterrorism Partnership.

Question. What is the outlook for a post-Bouteflika political class in Algeria? Is an eventual transition of power to a new generation of leaders likely to have an adverse impact on economic and security cooperation?

Answer. The United States supports the Algerian people and their democratic process. We have a productive partnership with President Bouteflika and the Government of Algeria, but it is for the Algerian people to decide who leads Algeria. The Algerian Constitution does not preclude Bouteflika from running for another term. We will continue to expand U.S.-Algerian cooperation across security and civilian sectors with President Bouteflika, or any other democratically elected leader.

LIBYA

Question. Libya remains fragmented, and the prevalence of armed militias prevents the central government from exercising its authority over the entire country. Rebel militias in Eastern Libya have even formed their own oil company and control several production and transportation facilities.

♦ What is the status of Libya's political transition, and prospects for new elections?

Answer. In elections viewed both domestically and internationally as credible and largely peaceful, Libyans elected a General National Congress in July 2012. PM Zeidan's government was approved by the GNC in October 2012. While the government enjoys democratic legitimacy, it lacks the ability to project its authority across the country or fulfill many core government functions. The government has found it difficult to implement reforms necessary to ensure a successful transition in part due to scant institutional capacity, day-to-day security challenges, and political power struggles.

In this context, the Libyan Government is still making halting progress executing its mandate to usher in full democracy. Preparations are ongoing for elections for the constitutional drafting assembly that may be held in January 2014. HNEC announced candidates could self-nominate in October, and 700 candidates registered by mid-November, including 74 women. After this body is elected, it will draft a constitution that will be put before popular referendum and serve as the basis for electing a permanent government, possible in mid- to late-2015.

Question. What is the status of plans to use funds from the Global Security Contingency Fund and other DOD programs to provide security assistance to the Libyan Government?

Answer. Through GSCF, over the next 3 years we (working with DOD) intend to assist the Libyan Government in creating an accountable, interministerial border security capability, including a border security force that upholds internationally accepted human rights standards while effectively defending Libya's borders against terrorism, weapons proliferation, and illicit trafficking. Our assistance will focus primarily on Libya's southern land border via an interagency approach. The program will focus on building capacity through the provision of technical expertise and training, and some equipping. We expect the Libyans to cover a number of costs.

For GSCF lines of effort under the Department of State, we are in the process of finalizing curriculums and training locations, in addition to working with the Libyan Government to identify the MOD, MOI, and Customs border security-related officials who will receive the training. We expect the first training under GSCF to take place in January, 2014.

The Department of Defense is implementing other GSCF programs.

Question. What resources, if any, do you expect will be needed for such programs over the next several years?

Answer. It is in our national interest to ensure Libya becomes a stable and democratic partner capable of addressing regional security challenges and advancing our shared interests. Our security assistance aims to address some of the most significant challenges to the democratic transition, including terrorism, porous borders, independent militias, and weak security and justice institutions. Our largest initiative, training general purpose forces, will be financed using Libyan funds; however the Libyan Government, plagued by weak institutions and limited capacity, faces difficulties spending its money effectively and focusing on many challenges at once.

While Libya is a wealthy nation, it requires technical assistance and advice from the United States and other partner nations. We should continue to provide support that builds the capacity of Libyan institutions to tackle challenges of greatest interest to the United States. We view our assistance in these areas as seed money intended jump-start Libyan Government investment in programs that ultimately the government must own. Over the next several years we will continue to evaluate needs in Libya with respect to our priorities, which will help inform programmatic and funding decisions.

Question. Please provide an update on the effort to train and develop a small core for a new Libyan Army. Who are we working with on this effort, and will this force be more of a protective force or will it have a broader security mandate?

Answer. To improve the government's ability to establish stability throughout the country, we responded positively to a request this spring from Zeidan that we train a General Purpose Force (GPF), the core of a new Libyan Army. We leveraged this bilateral commitment to encourage Libya's European partners to contribute to this effort. Libya plans to use their trained forces to provide basic protection for the Libyan Government and its institutions. At the U.K.-hosted G8 summit in June, we pledged to train 5,000–8,000 member general purpose forces and the U.K. and Italy also pledged to train 2,000 members each. Turkey has more recently pledged to train a similar number. The general purpose forces are expected to protect the Libyan Government and its institutions.

We plan to conduct the U.S.-led training in Bulgaria. We are discussing with the Libyan Government the many details required to implement this program, and coordinating with the U.K., Italy, Bulgaria, Turkey and Libya, and the U.N. Other bilateral and multilateral efforts to assist Libya with defense institution-building complement GPF training efforts.

The Libyan Government will pay for our contribution to the GPF effort through a Foreign Military Sales case, and training could begin as early as spring 2014. This program is currently in the development phase and we will provide further details when available.

RESPONSES OF DEPUTY ASSISTANT SECRETARY AMANDA DORY TO QUESTIONS SUBMITTED BY SENATOR ROBERT MENENDEZ

SMART POWER

Question. What bilateral and regional tools and pressure is the administration using to combat the destabilizing effects of extremist groups such as al-Qaeda in the Islamic Maghreb (AQIM)?

Answer. Combating violent extremist groups, such as AQIM, is a priority for the administration. The Trans-Sahara Counterterrorism Partnership (TSCTP) is the U.S. Government's multiyear, interagency, regional program designed to build the capacity and resilience of the governments and communities in the Sahel and Maghreb regions of Africa to contain, degrade, and ultimately defeat the threat posed by al-Qaeda, its affiliates, and other violent extremist organizations (VEOs) in the Trans-Sahara region. The TSCTP also provides a platform to improve regional and international cooperation and information-sharing, including between the Sahel and Maghreb regions, to counter shared threats. TSCTP partner countries include Algeria, Burkina Faso, Chad, Mali, Mauritania, Morocco, Niger, Nigeria, Senegal, and Tunisia.

The TSCTP budget request for FY 2014 is $45 million. These funds would enable us to build capacity and assist regional counterterrorism (CT) efforts across a large and diverse geographical area with complex security situations. Areas of support include: (1) enabling and enhancing the capacity of North and West African militaries to conduct CT operations; (2) integrating the ability of North and West African militaries, and other supporting partners, to operate regionally and collaboratively on CT efforts; (3) enhancing individual nations' border security capacity to monitor, restrain, and interdict terrorist movements; (4) strengthening the rule of law, including access to justice, and law enforcement's ability to detect, disrupt, respond to, investigate, and prosecute terrorist activity; (5) monitoring and countering the financing of terrorism (such as that related to kidnapping for ransom); and (6) reducing the limited sympathy and support among communities for violent extremism. Additionally, the United States supports countries in the region through bilateral International Military Education and Training (IMET) programs, which seek to help professionalize their respective militaries, and training and equipment funded from Foreign Military Financing (FMF), which often supports or sustains the capacity of foreign militaries toward achieving counterterrorism goals.

Other programs aimed to combat AQIM and other VEOs include the Department of State's Antiterrorism Assistance (ATA) program, which provides capacity-building programs for law enforcement agencies of partner nations. DOD has contributed to this through the 1206 program which has enhanced the capability of our North African partners to conduct CT operations.

With the growing youth population and burgeoning unemployment in the region, the United States also supports initiatives that deter youth from participating in terrorist networks, through programs designed to counter violent extremism (CVE). These programs provide positive alternatives to communities most at risk of recruitment and radicalization to violence, through providing educational opportunities and job trainings, and addressing specific drivers of radicalization narratives and the violent extremist worldview; and by promoting nonviolent interpretations of Islam.

TUNISIA

Question. The national dialogue, in which all parties have committed to participate in drafting a new constitution and electoral law and selecting an interim government to prepare new elections, has stalled over disagreements concerning the choice of Interim Prime Minister. All parties remain committed to the dialogue, but the 4–6 week timetable for the dialogue is very ambitious.

◆ What types of U.S. assistance, security and otherwise, have been most effective since 2011 in addressing Tunisia' security challenges and promoting economic and political reform, and an active civil society?

Answer. U.S. security assistance to Tunisia since 2011 has focused on supporting the Government of Tunisia's counterterrorism and counternarcotics efforts within the Trans-Sahara Counterterrorism Partnership (TSCTP) framework, and improving Tunisia's ability to secure its land and maritime borders. The Tunisian military receives the most U.S. Foreign Military Financing in Africa (other than Egypt), and a significant portion of Tunisia's military equipment is U.S. origin.

MOROCCO

Question. Our relationship with Morocco is strong, and it is the only country on the African Continent with which we have a Free Trade Agreement. The unresolved Western Sahara dispute is a barrier to further economic and security cooperation in the region.

◆ How does the administration plan to develop and deepen the 2012 Strategic Dialogue with Morocco?

Answer. The U.S. Government continues to support the process led by U.N. Secretary General Ban Ki moon and his Personal Envoy for Western Sahara, Christopher Ross, to find a peaceful, sustainable, and mutually agreed solution to the Western Sahara conflict. Ambassador Ross' work to bring the two parties together continues to hold promise and inspires hope for progress toward the resolution of this conflict, and it is these types of important issues that comprise the substance of the State Department-led Strategic Dialogue with Morocco. The United States supports Ambassador Ross' approach of bilateral talks with the parties with the aim to launch shuttle diplomacy to work toward finding a just, lasting, and mutually acceptable political solution.

Question. How might the U.S. support a more active Moroccan role in addressing regional security threats? Please describe the state of security cooperation with Morocco date and plans to strengthen this partnership.

Answer. Morocco and the United States have strong military ties, as evidenced by our annual U.S.-Morocco Defense Consultative Committee meetings, the eighth of which is scheduled for December 12. In addition, Morocco hosts the annual Exercise African Lion, which is DOD's largest military exercise in Africa and has expanded to include regional participants. The United States is very supportive of Morocco's willingness to expand its regional security cooperation efforts in Africa. Most recently, Morocco agreed to deploy its military to the Central African Republic to provide security for N forces in Bangui. We continue to encourage the Government of Morocco to engage with countries in the region in pursuit of our common security objectives.

ALGERIA

Question. The administration has encouraged Algeria to take a greater role in regional security efforts in the Sahel, including in Mali since 2012. Algeria's political culture remains dominated by the same ruling National Liberation Front generation of leaders who took over at independence in 1962. President Abdelaziz Bouteflika's health has deteriorated dramatically in 2013, and Presidential elections are due to take place in spring 2014, possibly pushing for a fourth term for Bouteflika.

◆ What steps has the administration taken to encourage greater political and eco- nomic openness in Algeria?
◆ How can we best support Algeria as it takes a larger regional lead in security and counterterrorism efforts?

Answer. The United States seeks to expand its security cooperation with the Algerian Government to enable it to strengthen its domestic and regional defense capabilities to counterterrorism and transnational trafficking in order to deny safe heaven to al-Qaeda and other violent extremist organizations. To that end, DOD engagements have focused on supporting Algeria's participation within the Trans-Sahara Counterterrorism Partnership (TSCTP) framework, expanding military-to-military engagements in areas such as border security, Counter-Improvised Explosive Device (C–IED), and air defense, and inviting Algerian military observers to U.S.-sponsored exercises such as AFRICAN LION and FLINTLOCK. The U.S. International Military Education and Training (IMET) program provides a number of positions for the training of younger Algerian military officers. DOD does not anticipate that a new generation of military leaders will significantly alter U.S.-Algeria military-to-military relations.

LIBYA

Question. Libya remains fragmented, and the prevalence of armed militias prevents the central government from exercising its authority over the entire country. Rebel militias in Eastern Libya have even formed their own oil company and control several production and transportation facilities.

◆ a. What is the status of Libya's political transition, and prospects for new elections?

Answer. In elections viewed both domestically and internationally as credible and largely peaceful, Libyans elected a General National Congress in July 2012. Prime Minister Zeidan's government was approved by the GNC in October 2012. Although the government enjoys democratic legitimacy, it lacks the ability to project its authority across the country or fulfill many core government functions. The government has found it difficult to implement reforms necessary to ensure a successful transition in part due to scant institutional capacity, day-to-day security challenges, and political power struggles.

◆ b. What is the status of plans to use funds from the Global Security Contingency Fund and other DOD programs to provide security assistance to the Libyan Government?

Answer. Through Global Security Contingency Fund (GSCF), over the next 3 years DOD (working with DOS) intend to assist the Libyan Government in creating an accountable, interministerial border security capability, including a border security force that upholds internationally accepted human rights standards while contributing to the defense of Libya's borders against terrorism, weapons proliferation, and illicit trafficking. Joint DOD/DOS assistance will focus primarily on Libya's southern land border through an interagency approach. The program will focus on building capacity through the provision of technical expertise and training, as well as equipping of a 150-member border security company. Given the difficult security situation in Libya, DOD may conduct training in a third country. We expect the Libyans to cover a number of costs, such as vehicles.

◆ c. What resources, if any, do you expect will be needed for such programs over the next several years?

Answer. It is in our national interest to ensure Libya becomes a stable and democratic partner capable of addressing regional security challenges and advancing our shared interests. Our largest initiative, training general purpose forces, will be financed using Libyan national funds via Foreign Military Sales cases; however, the Libyan Government, plagued by weak institutions and limited capacity, faces difficulties spending its money effectively and focusing on many challenges at once.

Although Libya is a wealthy nation, we should continue to provide support that builds the capacity of Libyan institutions to tackle challenges of greatest interest to the United States and jump-start Libyan Government investment in programs that benefit both the United States and Libya. Over the next several years we will continue to evaluate needs in Libya with respect to our priorities, which will help inform programmatic and funding decisions.

◆ d. Please provide an update on the effort to train and develop a small core for a new Libyan Army. Who are we working with on this effort, and will this force be more of a protective force or will it have a broader security mandate?

Answer. To improve the Libyan Government's ability to establish stability throughout the country, we responded positively to Prime Minister Zeidan's request to train a General Purpose Force (GPF) that would form the core of a new Libyan Army and provide basic protection for the Libyan Government and its institutions. Libya's European partners are also contributing to this effort. At the U.K.-hosted G–8 summit in June, DOD pledged to train 5,000–8,000 GPF personnel while the U.K. and Italy also pledged to train 2,000 members each. Turkey has recently signed a bilateral agreement to train approximately 3,000 Libyan personnel. The U.S.-led training is expected to occur at the Novo Selo Training Area, Bulgaria. DOD is discussing with the Libyan Government the many details required to implement this program, and are coordinating closely with the U.K., Italy, Bulgaria, Turkey, Libya, and the U.N. The GPF's primary function will be the protection of Libya's political, economic, and security institutions through security operations to include area security and border security. Training could begin as early as spring 2014.

www.ingramcontent.com/pod-product-compliance
Lightning Source LLC
Chambersburg PA
CBHW080538290526
45790CB00006B/2452